REVOLT AGAINST THE SUN

REVOLT AGAINST THE SUN

THE SELECTED POETRY OF
NĀZIK AL-MALĀ'IKAH

A Bilingual Reader

Edited and translated by
EMILY DRUMSTA

SAQI

Saqi Books
26 Westbourne Grove
London W2 5RH
www.saqibooks.com

Published 2020 by Saqi Books

ISBN 978 0 86356 317 1
eISBN 978 0 86356 352 2

A full CIP record for this book is available from the British Library.

Typesetting and design by Stuart Brown

Printed and bound by Clays S.A.r, Elcograf

CONTENTS

INTRODUCTION

Emily Drumsta

Nāzik al-Malā'ikah (1923–2007) was one of the most significant Arab writers of the twentieth century. Over the course of her career, she published seven poetry collections, four full-length works of literary criticism, and dozens of articles in the most widely read Arabic literary periodicals of the time. Yet for decades, to read Malā'ikah in English translation was to go hunting through anthologies of Arab women's poetry, seeking out a few poems here and there. By contrast, nearly every collection Maḥmūd Darwīsh ever wrote has been published as its own volume in English, and readers can peruse several books of Adūnīs' poetry in English too. Though equally as significant to the development of Arab modernism, women poets like Malā'ikah and her contemporaries Fadwā Ṭūqān, Lamī'ah 'Abbās 'Amārah, Mayy Ṣāyigh, and many others have for years been relegated to the realm of anthologies.

The significance of Nāzik al-Malā'ikah's poetry lies in the way each poem tells two stories at the same time. The first story relies on reference and association; it's what the poem is ostensibly *about*. The second story emerges in the sound of the poem as it sonically unfolds. And where the poem's narrative content leads us on a journey of the mind, its sound leads us on a journey of the senses, carrying us with its music.

For al-Malā'ikah, poetry and music are inseparable, and musical metaphors can be found throughout her writing, both in her poetry and critical essays. Although she is best known as a pioneer of 'free verse' poetry in Arabic, Malā'ikah remained fervently committed to the unique features of Arabic metrics throughout her career. 'The poetic feet have their roots in music,' she wrote in the landmark critical study *Issues in Contemporary Poetry* in 1962, 'and they are as stable and fixed in any language as numbers are in math.'[1] Indeed, nearly every time the word 'meter' (*al-wazn*) appears in *Issues*, musical terminology is not far behind. 'Meter is the soul that electrifies literary material and transforms it into poetry,' she writes. 'Indeed, images and feelings do not become poetic, in the true sense, until the fingers of music touch them and the pulse of meter beats in their veins.'[2] Poems with musical titles abound in nearly all of her collections, including 'songs' (*ughniyyāt*), 'hymns' (*anāshīd*), 'melodies' (*alḥān*), and 'tunes' (*naghamāt*), extending all the way through the poems 'Journey along the Strings of an Oud,' from *For Prayer and Revolution*, and 'The Symphony of Carpets,' from *The Red Rose*. And when Malā'ikah was asked to publish her 1977–79 Kuwait University lectures on Arabic metrics, including an essay titled 'The Secret of Poetic Music,' she titled the collection *The Music of Poetry*.[3]

Reading the many published biographies of Malā'ikah, it is not difficult to understand why music was so important to

---

1   In the same passage, Malā'ikah also compares poetic meter to a 'rainbow' insofar as 'the colors [in a rainbow] remain forever fixed; all the innovative painter does is mix these colors and change how he puts them on the canvas, blends them, and paints images with them.' Nāzik al-Malā'ikah, *Qaḍāyā al-Shi'r al-Mu'āṣir* [Issues in Contemporary Poetry], in *al-A'māl al-Nathriyyah al-Kāmilah* [The Complete Prose], vol. 1 (Cairo: al-Majlis al-A'lā li-l-Thaqāfah, 2002), 94.

2   Malā'ikah, *Qaḍāyā*, 197. For an analysis of *ṭarab* – that is, 'joy, rapture, entertainment (with music and the like)' – and its role both in Arab nationalism and Malā'ikah's work, see Robyn Creswell, 'Nazik al-Mala'ika and the Poetics of Pan-Arabism,' *Critical Inquiry* 46 (Autumn 2019): 90–93.

3   Nazik al-Mala'ikah, *Mūsīqā al-shi'r: Muḥāḍarāt* (Kuwait: Mu'assasat Jā'izat 'Abd al-'Azīz Sa'ūd al-Bābiṭayn li-l-Ibdā' al-Shi'rī, 2003). The essay is titled 'Sirr al-Mūsīqā al-Shi'riyyah.'

her theory and practice of poetry. Born in 1923, Malā'ikah was the eldest of seven children in the family of Ṣādiq and Salīmah al-Malā'ikah (also known as Salmā and, later, as Umm Nizār), both of whom were poets in their own right. According to one account, Nāzik began playing the oud at a very young age and composed her earliest poems as the lyrics to songs performed during social gatherings at the Malā'ikah family home, in the well-to-do Karrādah neighborhood of Baghdad.[1] Malā'ikah herself also describes having learned and internalized the rhythms of Arabic poetry not only through formal schooling, but also in time with the rhythms of her mother's household chores. 'In my childhood,' Malā'ikah writes, 'I would often hear my mother accompanying her housework with the poetry of Jamīl Buthaynah, Kuthayyir 'Azzah, Qays ibn al-Mulawwaḥ, al-Sharīf al-Raḍī, Abū Firās al-Ḥamadānī, Ibn al-Fāriḍ, al-Bahā' Zuhayr, and others.'[2] This may sound like a rose-tinted memory, but Malā'ikah was not the only writer to reflect on how classical Arabic poetry gave rhythm and form to the traditionally feminine tasks of housework: her contemporary, the Palestinian poet Fadwā Ṭūqān, also remembers 'performing household tasks with a poem in my pocket' and 'memorizing poetry while I ironed my brothers' shirts and trousers, while I made the beds, and while I washed the naphtha glass tops and filled the lamps with fuel.'[3] Though Malā'ikah likely exaggerated these and other stories about her childhood for effect, the portrait she paints of a family home where love ghazals, Sufi odes, and poetry from the Abbasid Golden Age mingled with housework, parties, and crowded Ashura

---

1   See Ḥayāt Sharārah, *Ṣafaḥāt min Ḥayāt Nāzik al-Malā'ikah* [Pages from the Life of Nāzik al-Mala'ikah] (London: Riyāḍ al-Rayyis, 1994), 11–71.

2   Nāzik al-Malā'ikah, 'Introduction,' in Umm Nizār al-Malā'ikah, *Unshūdat al-Majd* [Song of Glory] (Baghdad: Maṭba'ah al-Taḍāmun, 1968), 7.

3   Fadwa Tuqan, *A Mountainous Journey: An Autobiography*, trans. Olive Kenny (Saint Paul, MN: Graywolf Press, 1990), 64.

gatherings aptly conveys how she understood her own literary formation. Poetry, music, and the culturally specific rhythms of Arabic verse, she implies to her biographers, have been in her blood almost since birth, inherited from her literary parents and imbibed with the rhythms of daily life. Every account she gives of her life underscores the importance of these meters to her very being.

Given Malā'ikah's longstanding interest in the ties between musical and poetic composition, it is no surprise that she dedicated one of her major works of literary criticism, *The Monk's Cell and the Red Balcony* (1965), to the Egyptian Romantic Poet 'Alī Maḥmūd Ṭāhā, who is best known for his 'highly developed sense of music.'[1] In a fashion typical of her practical criticism, Malā'ikah eschews what she calls the 'vague language of "ringing" (*ranīn*) and "incandescence"' (*tawahhuj*) that saturates other scholars' criticism on Ṭāhā, developing instead specific, descriptive terms to show how Ṭāhā plays with alliteration and Arabic morphology to achieve his particular form of poetic music. Even in her criticism, then, Malā'ikah was as interested in identifying 'the secret of a poem's music' as she was in parsing its thematic content.[2]

Despite this longstanding interest in meter and music,

---

1   M.M. Badawi, *A Critical Introduction to Modern Arabic Poetry* (Cambridge, UK: Cambridge University Press, 1975), 137. See also Nāzik al-Malā'ikah, *al-Ṣawmaʻah wa-l-Shurfah al-Ḥamrā': Dirāsah Naqdiyyah fī Shiʻr 'Alī Maḥmūd Ṭāhā* [The Monk's Cell and the Red Balcony: A Critical Study of 'Alī Maḥmūd Ṭāhā's Poetry], in *al-Aʻmāl al-Nathriyyah al-Kāmilah* [The Complete Prose Works], vol. 2 (Cairo: al-Majlis al-Aʻlā li-l-Thaqāfah, 2002). Malā'ikah wrote the book in response to an invitation from the Supreme Institute of Arab Studies in Cairo to deliver a series of lectures on a topic of her choosing. Although the Institute suggested she speak about her experience as a poet, Malā'ikah, in the introduction to the book's second edition, remembers, 'apologizing because I preferred not to enter a lecture hall and lecture students about myself.' She chose to lecture about one of her favorite poets, 'Alī Maḥmūd Ṭāhā, instead.

2   Malā'ikah, *Ṣawmāʻah*, 120.

Malā'ikah's legacy in the world of Arabic letters is built on her
reputation as the pioneer of a specific poetic form, known in
Arabic as *al-shiʿr al-ḥurr* and in English, somewhat misleadingly,
as 'free verse'. Far from 'free' of metrical regularity, *al-shiʿr al-*
ḥurr isolated the Arabic metrical 'foot', or *tafʿīlah*, as the most
basic unit of sound in Arabic poetry. The traditional Arabic
poetic line generally consists of two hemistichs separated
by a caesura. Some meters combine two different feet in
alternating patterns, while others repeat the same foot three
or four times per hemistich. When written down, these poems
generally look like two columns laid on the page, leading many
modernists to describe them (often pejoratively) as 'columnar',
or *ʿamūdī*. In the 'free verse' poetry for which Malā'ikah would
become famous, by contrast, the poet chooses a single poetic
foot to repeat as many or as few times as desired in each line, in
accordance with the dictates of the poem's thematic content.
The base foot of the meter, however, had to remain the same –
on this point Malā'ikah insisted.

In the introduction to her 1949 collection *Shrapnel and*
Ash, Malā'ikah presented *al-shiʿr al-ḥurr* as a revolutionary,
radical departure from the Arabic meters systematized and
described by the lexicographer al-Khalīl ibn Aḥmad al-Farāhīdī
in the eighth century CE. 'We are still prisoners,' she wrote,
'held captive by the rules our forebears established in the
pre-Islamic and early Islamic periods ... gasping for air in our
poems, shackling our emotions in the chains of old meters and
creaking, dead expressions.'[1] However, with the publication
of *Issues in Contemporary Poetry* thirteen years later, Malā'ikah

1   Nāzik al-Malā'ikah, 'Muqaddimah' [Introduction] to *Shaẓāyā wa Ramād*
    [Shrapnel and Ash], in *al-Aʿmāl al-Shiʿriyyah al-Kāmilah*, vol. 1 (Cairo: al-Majlis
    al-Aʿlā li-l-Thaqāfah, 2002), 415. See also Nāzik al-Malā'ikah, 'Introduction to
    Shrapnel and Ash', trans. Emily Drumsta, in *Global Modernists on Modernism:*
    An Anthology, eds. Alys Moody and Stephen J. Ross (London: Bloomsbury
    Academic, 2020), 166–175.

seemed to have softened in her attitudes toward the traditional meters. 'The free verse movement', she wrote, emerged 'not from a desire to do away with traditional prosody (al-'arūḍ), but rather from an extreme *care* for prosody, which caused modern poets to notice the incredible uniqueness embedded in six of the Arabic meters and make these meters the bearers of a new metrical style, one which is built upon the old but adds something new and contemporary to it.'[1] Starting in the early nineteen-sixties, then, Malā'ikah's critical attitude toward 'free verse' had pivoted: the new style, epitomized in her own poem 'Cholera', was not a radical departure from a stifling tradition (as she had presented it in *Shrapnel and Ash*), but merely a reconfiguration of time-honored, authentically 'Arab' rhythms.

Malā'ikah carefully crafted, honed, and repeated the origin story of 'Cholera' over the course of her career, insisting on its status as a 'first' in order to seal her reputation as a modern metrical innovator, even though the poem is monostrophic rather than 'free'.[2] While she anticipated that the main resistance to *al-shi'r al-ḥurr* would come from Arab readers devoted to the monorhyme and regular rhythms of classical Arabic poetry, in the end Arab publics proved largely hospitable to the new form, having already encountered it in earlier poems by Ṭāhā, Jibrān Khalīl Jibrān, Niqūlā Fayyāḍ, Lūwīs 'Awaḍ, 'Alī Bākāthīr, and others who had 'broken the back of poetry' (to borrow 'Awaḍ's famous phrase) in the first half of the twentieth century.[3]

---

1   Nāzik al-Malā'ikah, *Qaḍāyā al-Shi'r al-Mu'āṣir* [Issues in Contemporary Poetry], in *al-A'māl al-Nathriyyah al-Kāmilah* [The Complete Prose Works], vol 1 (Cairo: al-Majlis al-A'lā li-l-Thaqāfah, 2002), 64.

2   See Creswell, 'Nazik al-Mala'ika,' and Shmuel Moreh, *Modern Arabic Poetry 1800–1970: The Development of its Forms and Themes Under the Influence of Western Literature* (Leiden: Brill, 1976), 198–215. 'Cholera' comprises four thirteen-line stanzas, each having a regular rhyme scheme and number of feet (*taf'īlāt*) per line.

3   Moreh, *Modern Arabic Poetry*, 196–215. On 'breaking the back of poetry', see Lūwīs 'Awaḍ, 'Ḥaṭṭimū 'Amūd al-Shi'r', in *Blūtūlānd wa-qaṣā'id ukhrā*

The greatest resistance to *al-shi'r al-ḥurr*, it turned out, would come not from those who wanted to maintain the classical forms, but from those who felt the new poetry did not go far enough to break with tradition. Ironically then, despite her emphasis on 'freedom' throughout *Issues* – and on all the ties between this Arabic word (*ḥurriyyah*) and political 'liberation' (*taḥrīr*) from colonial rule – Malā'ikah began to 'style herself as a present-day al-Khalīl',[1] a self-fashioning which landed her on the receiving end of virulent criticism from advocates of the 'prose poem' (*qaṣīdat al-nathr*) in Arabic. Standing by 'Cholera' as the standard against which all other formal experimentations were to be measured, Malā'ikah became known as a fierce defender of grammatical and metrical 'correctness' against the tides of what she considered to be dangerous poetic experimentation. Yūsuf al-Khāl's disparaging remark that Malā'ikah had 'donned the veil of conservatism and closed-mindedness' aptly sums up the reputation she came to have as a critic.[2]

---

min shi'r al-khāṣṣah (Cairo: al-Hay'ah al-Miṣriyyah al-'Āmmah li-l-Kitāb, 1989 [1947]), 9. The imperative Arabic phrase *ḥāṭṭimū 'amūd al-shi'r* can be interpreted in a number of ways: either as 'shatter the columns of poetry' (with reference to the 'columnar' shape of traditional poems on the page), or, in Huda J. Fakhreddine's translation, 'break the tent-pole of poetry' (with reference to the metrical language of Arabic, where lexical elements are referred to as 'cords' [*asbāb*] and 'pegs' [*awtād*]), or, in Levi Thompson's formulation, 'break the back' of poetry (since *'amūd faqrī* is the Arabic phrase for 'spinal column'). See Huda J. Fakhreddine, *Metapoeisis in the Arabic Tradition: From Modernists to Muḥdathūn* (Leiden: Brill, 2015), 71–74; and Levi Thompson, 'Speaking Laterally: Transnational Poetics and the Rise of Modern Arabic and Persian Poetry in Iraq and Iran' (PhD dissertation, University of California, Los Angeles, 2017), 1–6.

1   Robyn Creswell, *City of Beginnings: Poetic Modernism in Beirut* (Princeton: Princeton University Press, 2019), 121. In *Issues*, Mala'ikah writes: 'Just as al-Khalīl relied upon his poetic sensibility, his taste, and the Arabic poetry he had memorized to identify the meters of his time, so too have I relied on my poetic sensibility, my taste, and what I have memorized of Arabic poetry' (99–100).

2   Yūsuf al-Khāl, 'Qaḍāyā al-Shi'r al-Mu'āṣir, li-Nāzik al-Malā'ikah,' *Shi'r* 6, no. 24 (1962), 146. Cited in Creswell, *City of Beginnings*, 122. Translation by Creswell.

Perhaps the most virulent attack on Malā'ikah's formal conservatism, however, came from the Palestinian-Iraqi author and critic Jabrā Ibrāhīm Jabrā, who published his polemical response to *Issues*, 'Poetry and Ignorant Criticism', in 1963.[1] Unlike Malā'ikah, for whom 'free verse' was a modification of essentially Arab meters, music, and forms, Jabrā insisted 'the only examples and parallels capable of shedding light on modernist Arabic poetry must be found in the literatures and arts of the West, not of the Arab world.'[2] To explain the new currents of modernist innovation, Jabrā turns neither to al-Khalīl nor even to Jibrān or Ṭāhā, but rather to 'the history of poetry, painting and music in the West, from the Romantic revolution through whatever literary or artistic movement is currently in vogue in the cafés of Saint Germain-des-Près or the alleyways of London and Los Angeles.'[3] Though Jabrā does not dismiss the importance of the past in modernist innovation, still he argues that 'what Nāzik al-Malā'ikah wants from the past is restraint, as evidenced by her recourse to the meters of al-Khalīl and what she vaguely calls "the Arab instinct" (*al-fiṭrah al-'arabiyyah*) or "the Arab ear" (*al-udhun al-'arabiyyah*).'[4]

Unlike the 'free verse' poetry composed by Malā'ikah, her contemporary Badr Shākir al-Sayyāb, and others, the 'prose poem' had no allegiance to the Arabic poetic foot. Poets like Yūsuf al-Khāl, 'Unsī al-Ḥājj, Adūnīs, and others in the Beirut

---

1 Jabrā Ibrāhīm Jabrā, 'al-Shi'r wa-l-Naqd al-Jāhil' [Poetry and Ignorant Criticism], *Adab* 2, no. 1 (Winter 1963), 74–78. A revised version of the essay was later published as 'al-Shi'r al-Ḥurr wa-l-Naqd al-Khāṭi'' [Free Verse and False Criticism], in Jabrā Ibrāhīm Jabrā, *al-Riḥlah al-Thāminah: Dirāsāt Naqdiyyah* (Sidon: al-Maktabah al-'Aṣriyyah, 1967), 7–19. I cite from this revised version in what follows.

2 Jabrā, 'al-Shi'r al-Ḥurr wa-l-Naqd al-Khāṭi'', 9.

3 Jabrā, al-Shi'r al-Ḥurr wa-l-Naqd al-Khāṭi'', 9.

4 Jabrā, "al-Shi'r al-Ḥurr wa-l-Naqd al-Khāṭi',", 10. Note that this sentence specifically mentioning Malā'ikah is absent from the essay as it originally appeared in Adab in 1963.

circle of *Shi'r* magazine advocated – in theory and in practice – a form similar to English-language free verse: poetry whose rhythms, line-breaks, and layout on the page would be determined entirely by the poet's will, not by the dictates of classical poetic feet. Here music resided not in the undulations of long and short vowels pressed into the regular patterns of the *taf'īlah*, but in the rhythms of the poet's 'personal, private world.'[1] Malā'ikah was vehemently opposed to the prose poem, however, and she lashed out against its advocates at great length in *Issues*. 'Over the last ten years, a strange heresy (*bid'ah*) has spread through the literary climate in Lebanon,' she wrote.[2] She claimed to be distressed mainly by the *Shi'r* poets' application of the term 'poetry' (*shi'r*) to what was essentially 'prose' (*nathr*) with line-breaks, and she worried that this 'prose poetry,' which resembled *al-shi'r al-ḥurr* on the page, might 'confuse ordinary, everyday readers, who are not poets themselves and who may have very little background in Arabic poetry' into thinking there is no difference between the two.[3] This concern for the average Arab reader, however, hides a deeper disdain for European infiltrations into the Arabic poetic tradition. Malā'ikah referred to *Shi'r* as a magazine published 'in the Arabic language and the European spirit' and to her contemporaries as 'a generation that imitates Europe in everything, casting aside the rich and storied heritage of the Arabs.'[4] When citing the prose poetry of the Syrian Muḥammad al-Maghūṭ, meanwhile, she pointedly refused to reproduce its line-breaks. 'We will write this prose as prose should be written, with apologies to its author (whose excellent literary taste and originality have been damaged by

---

1 'Alī Aḥmad Sa'īd Isbir, "Fī Qaṣīdat al-Nathr," *Shi'r* 4, no. 14 (1960): 77.
2 Malā'ikah, *Qaḍāyā*, 189.
3 Malā'ikah, *Qaḍāyā*, 143.
4 Malā'ikah, *Qaḍāyā*, 191–192.

the artificial European spirit he has forcibly injected into his thoughts and expressions).'[1]

Given these and other examples of essentialism and dismissiveness in *Issues*, it is difficult not to agree with many of Jabrā's criticisms in 'Free Verse and Ignorant Criticism,' despite the condescension that saturates his essay. For one thing, as Jabrā points out, the language Malā'ikah used to write off poets who didn't strictly adhere to the formal standards of *al-shi'r al-ḥurr* was often unnecessarily cruel. At one point in *Issues*, she zeroes in on a poem by the Syrian-Lebanese poet Fu'ād Rifqah, which is technically composed in the *hazaj* meter but frequently breaks the line in the middle, rather than at the end, of a foot. Malā'ikah called the poem 'useless and without purpose' and urged that 'no critic should stay silent about such things,' since 'chaos and ugliness have limits.'[2] The syntax of the original Arabic – *inna li-l-fawḍā wa-l-qubḥ ḥudūd* – echoes the lyrics of 'Patience has Limits' (*Li-l-Ṣabr Ḥudūd*), a famous song by the Egyptian singer and pan-Arabist emblem Umm Kulthūm, of whom Malā'ikah was a great admirer. Even more significantly, as Jabrā also points out, the arguments advanced in *Issues* tend to rely too heavily on essentialisms such as 'the Arab instinct' or 'the Arab ear,' which land uncomfortably on contemporary ears.

To understand Malā'ikah's reliance on such essentialisms, we must revisit a key literary debate about modernity and tradition that rocked the Arab world in the nineteen-fifties and sixties. On one side of this debate, there were the poets and critics associated with *Shi'r* magazine in Beirut, who sought to launch Arabic poetry onto the stage of global modernism in part through the translation and implementation of European

---

1   Malā'ikah, *Qaḍāyā*, 190.
2   Malā'ikah, *Qaḍāyā*, 154. This section of *Issues*, titled "al-Shi'r al-Ḥurr wa-l-Jumhūr" [Free Verse Poetry and the Masses], was originally published in *al-Ādāb*, vol. 10 (October 1962): 3–6.

and American critical, theoretical, and poetic paradigms.[1] On the other side of this debate were figures like Malā'ikah, Suhayl Idrīs, and others associated with *al-Ādāb* magazine (also published in Beirut), who viewed European cultural incursions into Arabic poetry as extensions of the colonial and imperial systems of power whose hold over Arabic-speaking countries had, it was believed at the time, recently come to an end. Malā'ikah's *Issues*, though it has predominantly been read as a manifesto for *al-shi'r al-ḥurr*, can also be read as a manifesto of Arab nationalism in line with the views and principles held by this latter group.[2] Like many of her contemporaries invigorated by the rise to power of Gamal Abdel Nasser in Egypt, Malā'ikah countered colonial essentialisms with anti-colonial ones, revalorizing an Arab identity that had been studied, classified, and deemed lacking by generations of European colonial administrators and Orientalists. In the very last paragraph of *Issues*, Malā'ikah writes:

> Many of [our Arab critics] resolutely believe that we are less gifted than Western poets, and that we must be spoon-fed their theories if we want to develop Arabic poetry and criticism. I, on the other hand, would say that the material of our Arabic poetry and our Arab life is even richer and more fertile than the material of contemporary European poetry ... I would even predict that a sweeping wave of renewal will soon emerge from this Arab world of ours – one which will turn the West into pupils studying at the feet of our most gifted writers and critics. But this

---

1 For a thorough and engaging history of the magazine's development in the context of Cold War cultural politics, see Robyn Creswell, *City of Beginnings*.
2 Moreh makes a similar argument. See *Modern Arabic Poetry* 1800–1970, 272–273.

will only happen if we believe in ourselves ... Let us cease bending to the West. We are sick of French and English words in Arabic criticism. We are thirsty for local criticism whose keywords are derived from Arabic poetry itself, and in which Arab-ness (*al-'urūbah*) is the source of renewal. I call upon the new generation of critics to look inside themselves when they write, such that the fertile Arab mind might yield its fruit. Soon the nation will discover the true sources of its thought – those Arab sources in which the Arab critic will find all the richness and goodness he needs, without recourse to others.[1]

Read with critical, contemporary eyes, Malā'ikah's emphasis on the 'fertile Arab mind' (*al-dhihn al-'arabī al-khaṣīb*), its 'fruits' (*athmār*), and its 'true sources' (*al manābi' al-ḥaqq*) feel unsavory at best. Read historically, however, they reveal that there was more at stake in the free verse debates than line-breaks, rhyme schemes, and metrical feet. Malā'ikah and others, despite their reverence for John Keats, Lord Byron, and Thomas Gray, saw the incursion of European attitudes, terms and forms into Arabic literary criticism as little more than a continuation of colonial hegemony. Their Arabism was an anti-colonial political creation translated into aesthetic, formal terms.

If reverence for tradition and Arab nationalism were the bywords of Malā'ikah's reputation as a critic, as a poet, by contrast, she was known, particularly in her early collections, as the mistress of death, pain, and loss, a 'woman in love with night and all its lush ravines'.[2] Many studies of her poetry focus on its

---

1 Malā'ikah, *Qaḍāyā*, 281.
2 See my translation of 'Night Lover' ('Āshiqat al-Layl) in this volume. On the symbolism of 'night' in Malā'ikah's poetic works, see Jābir 'Uṣfūr, 'Ramziyyat al-Layl: Qirā'ah fī Shi'r Nāzik al-Malā'ikah' [The Symbolism of Night: A

sadness and pessimism, its treatment of death, its explorations of pain and suffering, and its fascination with night and darkness.[1] Malā'ikah's views on 'Poetry and Death' were clearly shaped by her studies of British Romantic poets in particular, both in Iraq and abroad.[2] After obtaining a bachelor's degree in Arabic language and literature from the Iraqi Teachers' Training College in 1944, she received a yearlong scholarship to study English at Princeton University and went on to earn a Master's degree in Comparative Literature from the University of Wisconsin, Madison.[3] Her first collection of poetry, *Night Lover*, published in 1947, contains an elegy for John Keats (included in this collection), a translation of Thomas Gray's 'Elegy Written in a Country Churchyard' (which Muhammad 'Abdul-Hai calls 'an Arabic romantic version of an essentially non-romantic poem'), and a partial translation of Lord Byron's 'Childe Harold's Pilgrimage'.[4] Meditations on death and life are

Reading of Nāzik al-Malā'ikah's Poetry], in *Nāzik al-Malā'ikah: Dirāsāt fī al-Shi'r wa al-Shā'irah* [Nāzik al-Malā'ikah: Studies on the Poet and Her Poetry], ed. 'Abdullah Aḥmad al-Muhannā (Kuwait: Sharikat al-Rabī'ān, 1975), 511–594.

1 See Yūsuf 'Aṭā al-Ṭarīfī, *Nāzik al-Malā'ikah: Ḥayātuhā wa Shi'ruhā* [Nāzik al-Malā'ikah: Her Life and Poetry] (Amman: Dār al-Ahliyyah, 2011), 89–101; Sālim Aḥmad Ḥamdānī, *Ẓāhirat al-Ḥuzn fī Shi'r Nāzik al-Malā'ikah:* [The Phenomenon of Sadness in Nāzik al-Malā'ikah's Poetry] (Mosul: Jāmi'at al-Mawṣil, 1980); Iḥsān al-Naṣṣ, 'al-Watr al-Ḥazīn fī Shi'r Nāzik al-Malā'ikah' [The Sad Streak in Nāzik al-Malā'ikah's Poetry], in *Nāzik al-Malā'ikah: Dirāsāt fī al-Shi'r wa al-Shā'irah*, 271–296; Ronak Hussein and Yasir Suleiman, 'Death in the Early Poetry of Nāzik Al-Malā'ika,' *British Journal of Middle Eastern Studies* 20, no. 2 (1993): 214–25; and Hanā' Muḥammad 'Abd al-Razzāq, 'Keats, Shelley and Byron in Nāzik al-Malā'ikah's Poetry' (Ph.D. diss., University of Glasgow, 1989), 201–214. 'Abd al-Jabbār Dawūd al-Baṣrī offers an excellent overview of the early Iraqi studies that painted Malā'ikah as a poet of death, night, and melancholy. See *Nāzik al-Malā'ikah: al-Shi'r wa al-Naẓariyyah* [Nāzik al-Malā'ikah: Poetry and Theory] (Baghdad: Dār al-Ḥurriyyah, 1971), 61–70.

2 See in particular the subsection 'al-Shi'r wa-l-Mawt' [Poetry and Death] in *Qadāyā*, 259–266.

3 'Abd al-Razzāq, 'Keats, Shelley and Byron,' 76.

4 Muḥammad 'Abdul-Hai, *Tradition and English and American Influence in*

plentiful in this collection, as are paeans to imagination and overflowing emotion, and poems composed in praise of night – all favorite topics among the British (and, subsequently, the Arab) Romantics.[1] Malā'ikah likely also imbibed a good deal of Romanticism through her in-depth study of Ṭāhā, who was famous for his translations of Shelley and, later in his career, for imbuing his strophic verses with passion and sensuality. Borrowing heavily from Keats in particular, Malā'ikah the poet – in contrast with Malā'ikah the critic – seems fascinated by the paradoxical connection between beautiful words and painful feelings. She understood poetry not only as a form of ornamentation or, in her words, 'fun luxury', but also as a performance of emotional work, 'an outlet for pain'.[2]

Both the form and the content of Malā'ikah's poetry bear the mark of Arab and British Romanticisms. On the level of content, the poems uphold overflowing feeling and deeply felt emotion as the heart of modern poetic expression. This emphasis on effect stands in sharp contrast with Arabic poetry's conventional role as the 'register of the Arabs' (*dīwān al-'Arab*), where poetry provided a kind of factual public record of major historical events in which heroic poets spoke on behalf of their tribes and communities. What distinguishes Malā'ikah's take on Romanticism from that of her male predecessors Ṭāhā and al-Shābbī, however, is the way she reformed the Romantics' emphasis on emotion into a distinctly feminist project,

---

Arabic Romantic Poetry: A Study in Comparative Literature (London: Ithaca Press, 1982), 27.

1   A section of *Issues in Contemporary Poetry* titled 'Poetry and Death' also links 'feeling' (*al-infi'āl*) with 'death' in the poetry of Abū al-Qāsim al-Shābbī, Muḥammad al-Ḥamsharī, John Keats, and Rupert Brooke. For Malā'ikah, Ḥamsharī and Shābbī were like Keats in that, for them, 'any event connected with [their] feelings necessarily reminded [them] of death ... For Keats, feeling was the goal of life itself. It is as though he were destined to be burned up with feeling so that he might become a great poet.' Malā'ikah, *Qaḍāyā*, 259–266.

2   See the headnote to 'Three Elegies for my Mother' in this volume.

recasting poetry as a space in which women could express emotion freely and authentically, without fear of retribution or accusations of 'shame' (*'awrah*).[1] Two essays from Malā'ikah's 1974 sociological study *Segmentation in Arab Society* directly address the double standards to which Arab women have historically been held. She upholds their right to become active members of modern, public life in these essays, while in her famous poem, 'To Wash off Disgrace', she critically denounces the practice of honor killing in the Arab world.[2]

On the level of form, meanwhile, the legacy of the British Romantics can also be felt – not in the 'free verse' for which Malā'ikah was famous, but in her strophic poems. Indeed, looking back over the entirety of her oeuvre, we might revise the story of Malā'ikah's significance to Arab modernism by shifting the emphasis away from *al-shi'r al-ḥurr* and onto the innovative stanza-forms she pioneered. Where her predecessor Ṭāhā experimented only infrequently with the stanza, rather than the line, as the basic unit of meaning in Arabic poetry, Malā'ikah frequently borrows stanza-forms from her favorite English poets, as in 'The Angry Wound', which, as she writes in the 'Introduction' to *Shrapnel and Ash*, 'is based on the

---

1   Creswell, 'Nazik al-Mala'ikah', 84–86. On how Malā'ikah's 'emancipation as an Arab woman' was connected to 'speaking rather freely and courageously about her feelings and emotions', see Wiebke Walther, 'From Women's Problems to Women as Images in Modern Iraqi Poetry', *Die Welt des Islams*, 36, vol. 2 (1996): 235.
2   See Nāzik al-Malā'ikah, 'al-Mar'ah Bayna al-Ṭarafayn: al-Salbiyyah wa al-Akhlāq' [Women Between the Two Sides: Passivity and Morals] and 'Ma'ākhidh Ijtimā'iyyah 'Alā Ḥayāt al-Mar'ah al-'Arabiyyah' [Social Observations on the Lives of Arab Women], in *al-A'māl al-Nathriyyah al-Kāmilah*, vol. 2, 481–492 and 493–507. Written in 1949, the poem 'Ghaslan li-l-'Ār' [To Wash off Disgrace] was first published in the journal *al-Adīb*, vol. 10 (October 1952): 3. It was later republished in the 1957 collection *Qarārat al-Mawjah* [At the Bottom of the Wave]. See *al-A'māl al-Shi'riyyah al-Kāmilah*, vol. 2, 103–104. For a translation, see Kamal Boullata, ed., *Women of the Fertile Crescent: Modern Poetry by Arab Women* (Washington, D.C.: Three Continents Press, 1978), 13–22.

innovative style used by the American poet Edgar Allan Poe in his innovative poem "Ulalume."[1] Some of Malā'ikah's most innovative stanza forms can be found in poems like 'I Am', 'Elegy for a Woman of No Importance', and, most significantly, 'Cholera'.[2] This last poem stands as a milestone less because of its 'freedom' and more for its ability to create images within such a tight rhetorical and metrical economy. Although earlier poets had already broken with the dual-hemistich 'columnar' form, it was Malā'ikah who perfected and solidified the regularly-rhymed, regularly-metered stanza as the new building block of modern Arabic verse. The 'free verse' of 'The Train Passed By' and other poems from *Shrapnel and Ash*, in other words, would not have been possible without the intermediary strophic forms of poems like 'Elegy for a Drowned Man', 'Revolt Against the Sun', and 'Trembling Melodies' from *Night Lover*.

Malā'ikah's reputation as a poet, then, was built on the eloquent, musical verses she dedicated to such topics as pain, suffering, darkness, night, and death. Less remarked upon in the voluminous criticism on her poetry, however, is the way these themes meld the interests of the British and Arab Romantics with gendered elements in pre-modern Arabic women's poetry. The most important of these elements is the association of women with the genre of elegy, or *rithā'*, stretching all the

---

1 Malā'ikah, 'Muqaddimah', to *Shaẓāyā wa Ramād*, in *al-A'mal al-Shi'riyyah al-Kamilah*, 16. The poem in question is 'al-Jurḥ al-Ghāḍib' [The Angry Wound].

2 'Anā' [I] and 'al-Kūlīrā' [Cholera] were published in *Shrapnel and Ash* (1949), while 'Marthiyyat Imra'ah lā Qīmata Lahā' [Elegy for a Woman of No Importance] was published in *Qarārat al-Mawjah* [At the Bottom of the Wave] in 1957. See Malā'ikah, *al-A'māl al-Shi'riyyah al-Kāmilah*, vol. 1, 481–482 and 498–500; and vol. 2, 54. For translations of 'I Am' and 'Insignificant Woman', see Boullata, *Women of the Fertile Crescent*, 13–22. Alternate translations of 'Elegy for a Woman of No Importance' and 'Cholera' are included in this volume.

way back to the pre-Islamic or *Jāhiliyyah* period.[1] Scholars have offered many explanations for the historical linking of women with elegy in Arabic poetry, ranging from the psycho-biological (women's 'emotional volatility' and 'weepy nature') to the socio-economic and ritual (the unavenged death of a kinsman creating a 'liminal' realm in which noblewomen, normally confined in pre-Islamic tribal society, were allowed to deliver public speech).[2] Marlé Hammond, meanwhile, argues that 'the success of women's [elegy] must lie partially in the aesthetic realm', particularly since 'this poetry was more than functional; it was high art, and considered as such, at least in the hands of its most cherished representatives'.[3] Hammond illustrates that women throughout the history of pre-modern Arabic literature composed 'not *what they could*, but rather *what they would,*' taking advantage of socially recognized poetic codes to express themselves in a range of modes and genres (*aghrāḍ*).[4] Despite the new perspective Hammond has offered us on the tradition, however, Malā'ikah and other women of her generation likely received and internalized the narrative of Arabic literary history that upheld elegy as a genre where female poets in

1   *Rithā'* is the name of the genre 'elegy'; *marthiyyah* refers to any example of a poem in the genre.
2   See Marlé Hammond, *Beyond Elegy: Classical Arabic Women's Poetry in Context* (Oxford, UK: Oxford UP, 2010), 48–49. The psycho-biological explanation of 'women's weepy nature' is from Mayy Yūsuf al-Khulayyif, *al-Shiʿr al-Nisāʾī fī Adabinā al-Qadīm* [Women's Poetry in Our Ancient Literature] (Cairo: Maktabat Gharīb, 1991), 52, and a similar explanation can also be found in Aḥmad Muḥammad al-Ḥūfī, *al-Marʾah fī al-Shiʿr al-Jāhilī* [Women in Pre-Islamic Poetry], 2nd rev. edition (Cairo: Dār al-Fikr al-ʿArabī, 1963). The analysis of elegy's 'ritual' function is from Suzanne Stetkevych, *The Mute Immortals Speak: Pre-Islamic Poetry and the Poetics of Ritual* (Ithaca, NY: Cornell UP, 1993), chapter 5.
3   Hammond, *Beyond Elegy*, 49.
4   Hammond, *Beyond Elegy*, 61. 'Genres' is perhaps not the best translation of the Arabic *aghrāḍ* (sing. *gharaḍ*), which can also mean 'intention', 'design', 'purpose', 'target', or 'mark', and which has a range of uses particularly in pre-modern Arabic letters.

particular excelled. In her memoirs, Fadwā Ṭūqān remembers her brother Ibrāhīm, himself a famous Palestinian poet, reading her an elegiac poem-fragment (qiṭ'ah) attributed to the female Jāhilī poet al-Salkah Umm al-Salīk in Abū Tammām's famous medieval anthology al-Ḥamāsah. 'I intentionally chose this poem for you', Ṭūqān remembers her brother explaining, 'so that you could see how Arab women have written beautiful poetry.'[1] Malā'ikah likely received a similar narrative about women poets in pre-modern Arabic poetry: their most 'beautiful' odes were also their saddest.

Yet the poetics of elegy in Arabic are not all weepy senti-mentalism and bereft longing. Elegy is also embedded with elements from other genres, including praise (madḥ), wisdom (ḥikmah), and incitements to war (taḥmīs) and blood venge-ance (taḥrīḍ). In the hands of pre-Islamic women poets, elegy was often a defiant genre, uttered in spaces that were both liter-ally and figuratively liminal.[2] In her poetry, Malā'ikah reclaims elegy, together with its companion themes of night, sadness, and overflowing, uncontrollable feeling, as privileged mecha-nisms for 'revolt' (thawrah). She plays on prominent pre-mod-ern examples in the genre to 'make it new'.

For me, the most important example of this play on tradition is 'Revolt Against the Sun', the poem which gives this collection its title. Though not explicitly an elegy, the poem nevertheless epitomizes this reclaiming of sadness, darkness, and melancholy as realms of 'revolt' (thawrah), with inevitable political undertones. It also subtly references the most famous elegy in Arabic poetry, in which the poet known as al-Khansā',[3]

---

1 Fadwā Ṭūqān, Riḥlah Jabaliyyah, Riḥlah Ṣa'bah [A Mountainous Journey], 2nd printing (Amman: Dār al-Shurūq, 1985), 68–69.

2 See Stetkevych, Mute Immortals, 165–166.

3 'al-Khansā' is a nickname meaning 'the snub-nosed'. The poet's full name was Tumāḍir bint 'Amr ibn al-Ḥārith ibn al-Sharīd. She was actually a mukhaḍramah poet, meaning her life spanned both the pre-Islamic and the

mourning her brother Ṣakhr, complained: 'I could not sleep, so I spent the night awake / as if my eyes were rubbed with grit // I watched the stars, though it was not my task to watch, / at times wrapping myself in my remaining rags.'[1] Like al-Khansāʾ, Malāʾikah affiliates herself with the 'night stars' in 'Revolt Against the Sun', asserting that they 'are the friends who guard me in the dark', and that they 'understand my spirit and my exploding feelings', guiding her through the night with 'threads of silver light'. In this line, 'night stars' (*nujūm al-layl*) is a non-human plural noun and should, according to the rules of Arabic grammar, behave as a feminine singular. But by referring to the stars as (female, human) 'friends' (*ṣadīqāt*), Malāʾikah allows them to act as a human plural, such that the stars become *hunna* (the Arabic pronoun for the plural feminine) and the verbs they perform (*yafhamna*, 'they understand,' *yuriqna*, 'they shine') are conjugated in the human feminine plural. The result is a dense semantic interweaving of night, darkness, and feminine community in the poetic speaker's defiant voice. 'Revolt' thus epitomizes much of Malāʾikah's larger project as a poet: displaying an implicit reverence for the Arabic poetic tradition (*tūrāth*) while also reconfiguring its tropes for a new audience of women speaking in similarly defiant tones.

A similar play on tradition also structures Malāʾikah's more straightforward elegies. Many of the most famous early Arabic elegies by women mourn the death of male kinsmen, from al-Khansāʾ's odes for her brother Ṣakhr to Suʿdā bint al-Shamardal's elegies for her brother Asʿad. Malāʾikah's elegies, by contrast, almost exclusively mourn *female* family members, from 'Three Elegies for my Mother' to 'For My Late Aunt' (all included in this collection). Malāʾikah also dedicates

early Islamic periods.

1   Geert Jan van Gelder, trans., *Classical Arabic Literature: A Library of Arabic Literature Anthology* (New York: NYU Press, 2012), 12–14.

several other, non-elegiac poems to women from her family, including a poem in rhymed couplets titled 'To My Sister Suhā' and another, 'The Moon Tree,' whose headnote describes it as 'a story I gave Maysoon when she was eleven'.[1] Numerous other elegies are devoted to unconventional and 'insignificant' subjects, including 'Elegy for an Unimportant Day', 'Elegy for a Woman of No Importance,' and 'Elegy for a Drowned Man' (a nod to the 'drowned Phoenician Sailor' in T.S. Eliot's 'The Waste Land'). The collections are also strewn with elegy-like poems for other subjects, including 'A Funeral for Happiness' and 'Cholera', in which the speaker mourns the victims of a 1947 epidemic of the disease in Egypt. In elegy, Malā'ikah seems to have found an ideal mode in which to play upon the figures and conventions of Arabic women's poetry, British Romantic poetry, and pan-Arab solidarity simultaneously.

In this sense, I would argue that it is impossible to divide Malā'ikah's career into an early, 'Romantic' phase and a later 'political' one. The early collection *Night Lover*, for all its explicit nods to Keats and its privileging of overflowing emotion, for example, also includes 'Revolt Against the Sun', with its explicit and implicit plays on political language (*thawrah*) and gender politics in the transmission and reception of classical Arabic poetry. Meanwhile, Malā'ikah's most explicitly political collections, *The Moon Tree* and *For Prayer and Revolution*, also include poems with Romantic reverence for nocturnal beauty, such as 'A Song for the Moon', and deeply personal poems such as 'A Letter from Him' and 'A Letter to Him'. By selecting and translating works from across Malā'ikah's long career, which is how I have presented her work here, I wanted to offer readers a glimpse at her versatility, her interest both in occupying the

---

1 Mala'ikah, *al-A'māl al-Shi'riyyah al-Kāmilah*, vol. 2 (Cairo: al-Majlis al-A'lā Li-l-Thaqāfah, 2002), 149.

traditional, pre-modern position of the poet as tribal spokes-
person and, at the same time, openly expressing deeply felt
emotions as a form of feminist defiance, a refusal to maintain
patriarchal distinctions between private and public spaces.

As a poet, Malā'ikah offers us an inventory of the past
infused with elements from the present, telling new stories
not by throwing away old forms, but by reassembling them in
a kind of linguistic and musical bricolage. Even as she brought
the stanza-forms and imagery of Romanticism into Arabic, her
poetry also responded to many of the most significant events of
the twentieth century in the Arab world, including the Second
World War, the Palestinian Nakba of 1948, the establishment of
the Iraqi Republic in 1958, the defeat of the Arab Forces in the
June War of 1967, and the Lebanese Civil War of 1975–1990.
In *Revolt Against the Sun*, readers can encounter Malā'ikah
both as the dreamy, defiant 'woman in love with night', and
as the fierce Arab-nationalist, anti-Zionist patriot proclaiming
her 'happiness with the Republic of Iraq' and warning her
Arab brethren that 'the abodes are being de-Arabized' and
'desecrated' by 'the footsteps of a foreign newcomer ... writing
"Tel Aviv" in the sands'.[1]

Beyond making a wider variety of Malā'ikah's work available
in English,[2] I also wanted to illustrate how she married
overflowing emotion with political occasion-marking in her
poetry throughout her career. In this vein, the 1959 triptych

---

1   See my translations of 'Taḥiyyah li-l-Jumhūriyyah al-'Irāqiyyah' [Greetings to
     the Iraqi Republic] and 'Ughniyyah li-l-Aṭlāl al-'Arabiyyah' [A Song for the
     Arab Ruins] (both from *The Moon Tree*) in this collection.
2   While a full bibliography of earlier translations of Malā'ikah's work is outside
     the scope of this introduction, see especially Salma al-Khadra al-Jayyusi's
     translations in *Modern Arabic Poetry: An Anthology* (New York: Columbia
     University Press, 1987), 329–338; Rebecca Carol Johnson's in *Fifteen Iraqi
     Poets*, ed. Dunya Mikhail (New York: New Directions, 2013); and Boullata,
     Women of the Fertile Crescent.

'Three Communist Songs' from 1968's *The Moon Tree* will be
of particular interest to readers of this volume. In these three
short poems, Malā'ikah satirically denounces the subservience
of Arab Communists to Soviet party policies at the expense of
what she views as more pressing Arab nationalist priorities.
'Beware, comrade,' she writes in a tone of arch irony. 'The
rose has religion / it smells Arab.' The poems should perhaps
be read alongside another trilogy from *The Moon Tree*,
'Three Arab Songs,' the first of which is titled 'The Hour' and
prefaced with a quote from Gamal Abdel Nasser: 'The hour of
revolutionary work is upon us.'[1] It is jarring but not surprising
to those familiar with modern Iraqi history that Malā'ikah
pivoted so rapidly from her 1958 celebration of the coup which
brought 'Abd al-Karīm Qāsim to power (and in which the Iraqi
Communist Party played a key part) to her denunciation of the
Communists in 'Three Communist Songs'. The second song's
characterization of Communists as bloodthirsty animals was
likely Malā'ikah's pan-Arabist critique of the violent role played
by the ICP in the Kirkuk protests of 1959.[2]

Malā'ikah was not alone in criticizing what she viewed as
the misaligned priorities of the Iraqi Communists in 1959.
That same year, fellow Iraqi modernist Badr Shākir al-Sayyāb
published a series of essays titled 'I Used to be a Communist'
in the Baghdad daily *al-Ḥurriyyah*.[3] Largely a response to the

---

1   The Arabic poem is titled 'al-Sā'ah' and the Nasser quote reads: 'Laqad daqqat
     sā'at al-'amal al-thawrī.'
2   On these protests, and Kurdish violence toward ethnic Turkmen in Kirkuk,
     see Hanna Batatu, *The Old Social Classes and the Revolutionary Movements
     of Iraq: A Study of Iraq's Old Landed and its Commercial Classes and of its
     Communists, Ba'thists, and Free Officers* (Princeton: Princeton University
     Press, 1978), 912–921; and Elliott Colla, 'Badr Shākir al-Sayyāb, Cold War
     Poet', *Middle Eastern Literatures* 18, vol. 3 (2015): 249.
3   On these essays their relationship to the Congress for Cultural Freedom, a
     cultural wing of the U.S. Central Intelligence Agency, see Colla, 'Badr Shākir
     al-Sayyāb', and Levi Thompson, 'An Iraqi Poet and the Peace Partisans:

violence in Kirkuk, in these essays Sayyāb publicly severed ties with his former colleagues in the Party and announced his new affiliation not with Communist Internationalism, but with pan-Arab nationalism. In the first of her 'Three Communist Songs,' Malā'ikah almost self-consciously fuses her reputation as a sad and dreamy Romantic with her satire of Communist conspiracy theories. 'Maybe the shadows are plotting a secret conspiracy / together with the starlight and the evening's still,' she writes. 'These hills, that road / this dark, they're all Agents.' Malā'ikah is often left out of critical conversations about Cold War alignments, pan-Arabist rhetoric, and Iraqi politics around the end of the nineteen-fifties, perhaps because of her 'feminine' reputation as the mistress of sadness and pain, or perhaps because of a persistent desire, among her Arab and Western critics, to preserve the pristine, poetic realm from the incursions of local and global politics.[1] But as 'Three Communist Songs,' 'A Song for the Arab Ruins,' and other poems from *The Moon Tree* and *For Prayer and Revolution* reveal, Malā'ikah, like her colleague Sayyāb, participated in local Iraqi, pan-Arab, and international debates about the proper place of Arab solidarities in Cold War politics. Whether intentionally or not, Malā'ikah, like Sayyāb, was a 'Cold War poet'.[2]

There were also creative reasons why I undertook this project. Specifically, I wanted my translations to reflect some, if not all, of the formal qualities that made Malā'ikah's Arabic originals so famous. Given that so much of her significance is built on her experiments with *al-shiʿr al-ḥurr*, and her fierce defenses of this form against the advocates of the prose poem, it

---

Transnational Pacifism and the Poetry of Badr Shākir al-Sayyāb', *College Literature* 47, no. 1 (2020): 65–88. I have not found any evidence that Malā'ikah had ties with the CCF.

1 Creswell's 'Nazik al-Mala'ikah and the Poetics of Pan-Arabism' is a notable recent exception.
2 Colla, 'Badr Shakir al-Sayyāb', 248.

seemed like an injustice to remain only with the literal meanings
of Malā'ikah's words, to make these carefully metered Arabic
creations into unmetered English ones. In many instances
throughout the poems collected here, it is clear that Malā'ikah
has taken liberties either to fill out the meter or to cinch the
rhyme. If music was so key to Malā'ikah's poetic project,
as *Issues in Contemporary Poetry* and her autobiographical
writings consistently affirm, why not take similar liberties to
make the music 'work' in English?

If Malā'ikah had taken part in the debates about
'foreignization' and 'domestication' among scholars of literary
translation, she would likely have been firmly on the side of the
latter, judging from several passages in *Issues*. She specifically
criticizes Jabrā and Fawwāz al-Ṭarābulsī for translating English
and French poetry into Arabic in a way that preserves the line-
breaks of the original but fails to respect the metrical rules of *al-
shi'r al-ḥurr*. 'It is not right,' she asserts, 'for everyday, ordinary
prose to be broken (*muqaṭṭā'*) into seemingly poetic lines like
this ... If the translator is dead-set on line-breaks (*al-taqṭī'*), he
should translate this foreign poetry into Arabic poetry, with
everything that implies: meter and rhyme as well as emotion
and imagery.'[1] Poetic translations, in Malā'ikah's view, should
adapt themselves to the rhythmic, metrical, and musical forms
of the target language. In an attempt to respect these views on
the translation of European poetry into Arabic, I have tried
to translate Malā'ikah's poetry in such a way that the English
meters reflect (or at least gesture toward) the regularity of her
original poems, even if they must do so in different ways.

The main challenge of *Revolt Against the Sun* lay in find-
ing English verse patterns that would translate the music of
the Arabic originals without compromising their images and

---

1   Malā'ikah, *Qaḍāyā*, 141–43.

metaphors. My first step with every poem was to do a literal translation: putting subjects and objects in their proper places, noting nuances of polysemy, and marking any instances of homonymy, paranomasia, antithesis, or other wordplay in Arabic. These literal translations then had to be set to meter and sometimes rhyme, and in this process, the vast differences between Arabic and English prosody became yet another obstacle. Arabic meters are quantitative – that is, based on patterns of long and short vowels undulating in regular modulations (hence the Arabic word *baḥr*, which translates both 'sea' and 'meter'). English meters, by contrast, are conventionally qualitative, based on patterns of stressed and un-stressed syllables. This form of accentual-syllabic verse, as John Hollander points out in a classic manual, 'involves such patterns as "iambic", "dactylic", etc., all somewhat confusingly named for Greek meters in a totally different system'.[1] English metrical feet, furthermore, are much shorter than the Arabic *tafʿīlāt*, offering only two or three syllables to the *tafʿīlah*'s four or five.[2]

At first, I was hoping to find a single system by which I would organize the line-patterns, meters, and stanza-forms of all the poems in *Revolt Against the Sun*. What I found, however, was that each poem necessitated its own solution, drawn from a series of strategies that I developed as I went. One strategy was to select key examples from the history of English poetry as models for the verse-forms of my translations. For the first of Malāʾikah's three elegies for her mother, 'A Song for Sadness', for example, I modeled the meter and stanza-form of my translation after one of the most famous elegies in modern English, 'In Memoriam A.H.H.,' by Alfred Lord Tennyson. Tennyson's poem is

---

1 John Hollander, *Rhyme's Reason: A Guide to English Verse*, 4th ed. (New Haven: Yale University Press), 5.
2 Some *tafʿīlāt*, however, are also quite short, as in the *mutaqārib*, the *mutadārik*, and the (rare) *muqtaḍab*.

composed of quatrains in iambic tetrameter rhymed *abba*, while Malā'ikah's Arabic poem consists of five six-line stanzas based on the *kāmil* meter, with the first four lines in tetrameter and the last two forming a trimeter couplet, all rhyming *abbaab*. My English version uses Malā'ikah's elegiac strophe to modify Tennyson's, adding a trimeter iambic couplet to the end of the quatrain and reproducing (in all but the couplet) the original rhyme scheme. Malā'ikah's 'The Moon Tree', meanwhile, is a narrative poem composed in couplets set to the *mutaqārib* or 'tripping' meter. Here the dramatic and narrative elements of the original drove me to look for English models with a similar history in narrative verse. I eventually landed on the storied heroic couplet, with its familiar iambic rhythm, and I relied in particular on Vladimir Nabokov's modernist take on this well-worn form in *Pale Fire* as a model. Meanwhile, in Malā'ikah's 'To the Poet Keats', the poetic speaker at one point cites directly from John Keats' 'Ode to a Nightingale', translating several of its famous lines into Arabic. I thus turned to Keats' liquid iambic rhythm as my metrical model for this work. These nods to English verse and lyric both provide familiar echoes for English-language readers and pay homage to Malā'ikah's own reverence for English language poetry.

In addition to finding English models that might render or reference the form, mood, and purpose of the Arabic original, I also had to develop an adequate English form for the many poems that Malā'ikah composes in classical, *'amūdī* structure. The musicality of these poems relies heavily on the break or breath that the caesura allows in Arabic. One of the most common ways English translators have dealt with this peculiarity of the Arabic line is through indentation: the single Arabic line is broken into two English ones, with the second indented as though it were an answer to the first. However, this solution felt unnatural for

Malā'ikah's verses, where there is often enjambment across the caesura and, as in some pre-modern Arabic verse, a sense of unity to the line itself. I was also curious to see if there was an English verse form that could somehow preserve the integrity of the single Arabic line, embedding a sonic caesura where there might not be a printed one. The solution I arrived at was the 'fourteener' or 'poulter's measure', once beloved by William Blake, which helpfully embeds a sonic pause between the fourth and fifth of its seven stresses.[1] 'For My Late Aunt' and 'A Funeral for Happiness' are both examples of poems written in classical Arabic meters (*kāmil* for the former; *al-mutaqārib* for the latter) that I've translated into English fourteeners. The imagery is so intricate in both poems (e.g. 'the hollow in your pillow: fallen planet in my heart;' 'face tilled and sown by stars and lustrous with their dappled light'), that I found it too cruel to force rhymes where they didn't arrive naturally. 'A Song for the Moon' offers a similar experiment with the fourteener in which imagery is key. The Arabic reads like an encyclopedia of moon metaphors, and I abandoned rhyme in the hopes that my English version would read the same way.

For poems built with 'tripping' meters (like the *mutaqārib* and the *mutadārik*), I relied on the anapest (two unstressed syllables followed by a stress) as my base foot. Beyond Lord Byron's famous 'The Destruction of Sennacharib', to my knowledge the only writers to use anapestic meters with any success in English have been composers of light verse and children's books, including Theodor Geisl (better known as Dr. Seuss) and famed 'nonsense poet' Edward Lear. Yet despite their perceived childishness, anapestic meters have long been used for narrative verse (from Byron all the way through *The Cat in the Hat*), and the anapest's horse-hoof-like quality (da-

---

1   This too I learned from Hollander, *Rhyme's Reason*, 13.

da-*dun*, da-da-*dun*) proved key to my version of 'Cholera'.[1] In *Issues*, Malā'ikah describes how, in 'Cholera', she had 'tried to express the rhythm (*waqʿ*) of the horses' hoofs as they pulled carts piled with dead victims of the epidemic across the Egyptian countryside'.[2] To recreate this galloping in English, I created a 'free anapestic meter' modeled on the parameters of *al-shiʿr al-ḥurr*. Some of the lines consist of only a single foot ('in the night,' 'in the dawn,' and the dactylic substitution 'cholera'), where others run to four and even five anapests long. To mimic the 'tripping' (*mutadārik*) of the poem's refrain, meanwhile (*al-mawt al-mawt al-mawt*), I changed the normally spondaic literal translation ('death death death') to the more galloping 'they are dead, they are dead, they are dead'. A regular anapestic meter also allowed me to replicate the *mutadārik* rhythm of 'To a Girl Sleeping in the Street'.

The question of how to carry over Malā'ikah's most famous form, *al-shiʿr al-ḥurr*, into English was perhaps the most pressing of all. In one painstaking experiment, I tried to replicate both the rhyme scheme and the irregular foot-pattern of the Arabic original. For 'The Path of Return' (*Ṭarīq al-ʿAwdah*), I created a map of sorts, marking how many feet were in each line and where they rhymed. I set a rule that if Malā'ikah used five feet in her Arabic line, I would use five iambs or anapests in my English one; if she used four, I'd use four, etc.; and if she rhymed *abbbccadefef*, I'd rhyme in the same pattern. Unsurprisingly,

---

1   Hollander's note on anapestic meter also influenced these decisions: 'There are rhythms like this that you'll frequently meet: / They resound with the pounding of regular feet, / And their anapests carry a narrative load / (The hoofbeats of horses, of course, on the road)', adding that they 'can seem either active or passively elegiac' (15–16).

2   Malā'ikah, *Qaḍāyā*, 304 (footnote n. 4 from p. 51). Note that this explanation appeared on the first page of the first edition of *Issues*, but Malā'ikah seems to have relegated it to a footnote in this later edition to clear space for a lengthy defense of her experiment as the very first. See Creswell, 'Nazik al-Mala'ika,' 76.

these constraints forced the literal meaning of the translation too far from the original, and I ultimately abandoned them. In their place, I used iambic meter in various line-lengths to recreate the rhythm of Malā'ikah's free verse poems. My lines, like Malā'ikah's, were also of varying lengths, though not necessarily in the same length-pattern as in the original Arabic. The iamb offered not only the most flexible but also the most natural base for this anglicized version of *shi'r ḥurr* in long poems like 'The Train Passed By,' 'Elegy for an Unimportant Day,' and 'Song of the Abyss'. Robert Hass argues (emphatically) that, because the English ear tends to organize unstressed syllables around stressed ones in a 'rising' pattern, *'almost all metrical poetry in English is written in an iambic meter or in a meter that has an iambic base.'* [1] Given these tendencies of speech, stress, and hearing, this variable iambic rhythm proved the most consistent form for recreating *al-shi'r al-ḥurr* in English.

Beyond the solutions I devised for rendering metrical experiments, the other, arguably more intractable translation problem I faced in *Revolt Against the Sun* was that of rhyme. Traditionally, Arabic odes are monorhymed, with a single rhyme sonically unifying sometimes hundreds of lines. Monorhyme was an issue of much debate among Malā'ikah's contemporaries, and Malā'ikah herself refers to rhyme as a 'beautiful, tyrannical queen sitting at the end of every line and insisting on being the most noticeable word in it'. [2] Nevertheless, most of Malā'ikah's

---

1   Robert Hass, *A Little Book on Form: An Exploration into the Formal Imagination of Poetry* (New York: Harper Collins, 2017), 400.

2   Malā'ikah, *Qaḍāyā*, 68. Malā'ikah further claims, in this passage, that rhyme is part of what made poetry a 'luxury' object in Arab courtly culture. 'Perhaps this feeling of opulence and emptiness is what saturates old poetry with atmospheres heavy with amber, zephyrs, and silk clothing dragged along by beautiful girls who have nothing to do all day besides pamper themselves and take noontime naps.' The contemporary poet, by contrast, is 'an individual in a society that works and builds', and he feels 'oppressed by this lazy, sleepy atmosphere, this heavily enforced aesthetic.'

poems do rhyme in some form or another, whether regularly (in her numerous strophic poems), or irregularly (as in the free verse poems), and these rhymes tend to land lightly and pleasantly in Arabic. Both the grammar of Arabic and the nature of rhyme in the language (a repeated consonant marked with the same vowel throughout) make rhyme a fairly easy way of organizing poetic sound. Rhyme in English, by contrast, is less common and more difficult. It tends to ring in modern ears as either dated or childish, more a thing of song (or rap, perhaps the last remaining realm where rhyme equates to prowess) than one of poetry. Here again, as with meter, I did the best I could. I strove for slant-rhymes where possible, to dampen the ringing (see, for example, 'Elegy for a Woman of No Importance,' 'Song of the Abyss,' 'A Funeral for Happiness'), and where a possible rhyme presented itself, I let it lie, even if not in the strict patterns or exact places of the original Arabic. For some poems, it seemed to me that rhyme was necessary to give readers of the English a similar experience to the one a reader of the Arabic verses might feel. After all, many of these poems are not all that experimental, and they are built this way by design. Why should the English verse be blank where the Arabic is not?

On a good day, I feel as if the formal experiments of these translations do something worthwhile for the translation of Arabic poetry, bringing Malā'ikah to new readers in a way that she might have appreciated and even respected. On a bad day, I fear these poems read as little more than English ditties, hardly improvements on the old Orientalists' metrical renderings of classical Arabic and Persian poetry, now confined to dusty tomes (and tombs). In his 1981 guide to English verse, Hollander reminds us that poetry 'is a matter of trope' while verse is one of 'scheme or design', and for this reason, 'most verse is not poetry'.[1] In a similar vein, Malā'ikah too once noted that 'every poet is a necessarily versifier, but not every versifier is a poet'.[2] I admit there were moments in this process where I felt more like a versifier than a poet, where I relied more on fingers tapping than on inspiration painting. If at times the verses that follow fail to live up to their Arabic counterparts, I take refuge in the idea that these experiments may have opened the door to others interested in moving beyond the merely literal, in translating something of the undulating Arabic music.

I also frequently return to a pair of pictures that I came across in my research. Printed in *Shi'r* magazine, the photos were taken in January 1960. In the first, eleven poets and critics sit together on a couch – Fadwā Ṭūqān, Nāzik al-Malā'ikah, Khālidah Saʿīd, and Laure Ghorayeb sit in their stylish sixties' suits alongside Shawqī Abī Shaqrā, Muḥammad al-Māghūṭ, Yūsuf al-Khāl, Fu'ād Rifqah, Adūnīs, Jūrj Ṣaydaḥ, and Badawī al-Jabal. The group was gathered, a caption informs us, for a session of the magazine's weekly Thursday reading series. A second picture follows, this one gathering only the women together on the same couch. I like to imagine the potential captions that might have run through the photographer's mind as he invited the poets to pose for a second photo, separate from the men. 'Arab women poets gather for a reading at *Shi'r* magazine.' 'Female pioneers share a moment in Beirut.' Nāzik, Fadwā, Khālidah, Salmā. They just laugh.

---

1   Hollander, *Rhyme's Reason*, 1.
2   Malā'ikah, *Qadāyā*, 197. In Arabic: *Kull shā'ir nāẓim bi-l-ḍarūrah, wa laysa kull nāẓim shā'iran.*

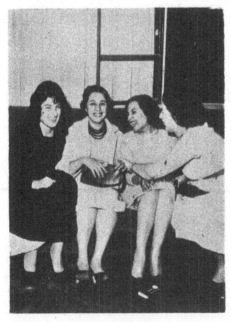

Above: A photo from *Shiʿr*, vol. 4, no. 13 (Winter 1960). The caption reads: "(From left to right) Front Row: Shawqī Abī Shaqrā, Muḥammad al-Māghūṭ, Yūsuf al-Khāl, Fuʾād Rifqah, Adūnīs, Fadwā Ṭūqān, Lūr Ghurayyib; Back Row: Jūrj Ṣaydaḥ, Nāzik al-Malāʾikah, Badwī al-Jabal, Salmā al-Khaḍrāʾ al-Jayyūsī. They were gathered for a session of *Shiʿr's* Thursday reading series in January, 1960."

Left: A photo from *Shiʿr*, vol. 4, no. 13 (Winter 1960). The caption reads: "(From Left to Right): Khālidah Saʿīd, Nāzik al-Malāʾikah, Fadwā Ṭūqān, Salmā al-Khaḍrāʾ al-Jayyūsī"

POEMS FROM
NIGHT LOVER
(1947)

قصائد من
عاشقة الليـل
(١٩٤٧)

Revolt Against the Sun

A GIFT TO THE REBELS

She stood before the sun, screaming out loud:
Oh Sun, my rebel's heart is just like you:
while young, it washed away much of my life,
its lights quenched the stars' thirst, ever renewed.
Careful, don't let the sadness in my eyes
or these copious tears deceive your sight.
This sadness is the form of my revolt,
to which the gods bear witness every night.

Careful, don't be deceived by my pale skin,
these quivering emotions, this dark frown.
If you see indecision, or the lines
of fierce poetic sadness on my brow,
know that it's feeling causing my soul's grief
and tears at life's terror – it's prophecy
that failed to fly, but stood up to resist
a life of sadness and melancholy.

ثورة على الشمس

هدية إلى المتمردين

وَقَفتُ أمام الشمس صارخةً بهـا
يا شمـسُ مثلُـكِ قلبـي المتمـرِّدُ

قلبي الـذي جَـرَفَ الحيـاةَ شبابُهُ
وسَقَى النجـومَ ضياؤه المتجـدِّدُ

مهـلاً ، ولا يخدعُـكِ حُـزنٌ حـائرٌ
في مقلـتيَّ ، ودَمعـةٌ تتنهّـدُ

فالحـزنُ صـورةُ ثـورتي وتمـرُّدي
تحـت الليـالي والألوهـةُ تَشهـدُ

مَهـلاً ولا يخدَعـكِ حـزنٌ مـلامحي
وشحـوبُ لـوني وارتعـاشُ عواطفي

وإذا لمحـتِ على جبيـني حَـيْرتي
وسُطورَ حزني الشاعريّ الجارِف

فهو الشـعورُ يُثـيرُ في نفسي الأسى
والدمعَ في هـول الحيـاةِ العاصفِ

وهي النبـوّةُ لم تطِـرْ فتمـرَّدَت
بالحُـزْنِ في وجهِ الحيـاةِ الكاسفِ

My lips are fastened shut over their pain,
my eyes are thirsty for sweet drops of dew,
the evening left its shadow on my brow
and morning's killed off all my pleas to you.
I came to pour out my uncertainty
in nature, amid fragrances and shade,
but you, Sun, mocked my sadness and my tears
and laughed, from up above, at all my pain.

Even you, Sun? Alas, what misery!
You were the one I yearned for in my dreams,
you were the one whose name I once revered,
singing the praises of your smiling beams.
You were the one I once held sacred and
idolized as a refuge from all pain.
But now, crusher of dreams, melancholy,
darkness, and shadows are all that remain.

I will shatter the idol that I built
to you out of my love for radiance
and turn my eyes away from your bright light –
you're nothing but a ghost, splendor's pretense.
I'll build a heaven out of hidden hopes
And live without your luminosity.
We dreamers know we hold within our souls
divine secrets, a lost eternity.

شَفَتايَ مُطبَقتـان فـوق أَساهـا
عينــايَ ظامِئتـانِ للأنـداءِ
تَـركَ المسـاءُ عـلى جبيـني ظِلَّهُ
وقضى الصبـاحُ على جديد رجائي
فأتيـتُ أسكُبُ في الطبيعـة حَيْرَتي
بـين الشَّـذى والـوردِ والأفيـاءِ
فَسَخِرتِ من حُزني العميقِ وأدمُعي
وَضَحِكـتِ فوق مـرارتي وشَـقائي

يا شمـسُ حتـى أنـتِ؟ يا كآبـتي!
أنـتِ التـي ترنـو لهـا أحـلامي
أنـتِ التـي غنَّى شَبابي باسمها
وشَـدا بفيـض ضيائهـا البسَّـام
أنـتِ التـي قدَّسـتُها وَتَّخَذتُهـا
صَنَماً ألـوذُ بــه مـن الآلآمِ
يا خيبـةَ الأحـلامِ، مـا أبقيـتِ لي
إلا ظــلالَ كآبـتي وظـلامي

سـأحطِّم الصنَمَ الذي شيَّدتُهُ
لـك مـن هَـوايَ لكـلِّ ضوءٍ ساطِع
وأديـر عينـيَّ عن سَناكِ مُشيحةً
مـا أنـتِ الّا طيفُ ضوءٍ خـادِع
وأصـوغ مـن أحـلام قلبي جنَّـةً
تُغَنّي حيـاتي عن سَناكِ اللامـع
نحـنُ الخياليّـيـنَ، في أرواحنـا
سـرُّ الألوهـةِ والخُلـودِ الضائـع

Do not spread out your beams over my grove,
You rise for other than my poet's heart.
Your light no longer stirs feelings in me,
the night stars now inspire all my art.
They are the friends who guard me in the dark,
they understand the feelings that ignite
my spirit, they extend thin, silver threads
to guide my eyes through the enchanted night.

Night is life's melody, its poetry,
here gods of beauty roam to their content,
here uninhibited souls fly about
and spirits hover in the firmament.
How often I have wandered to forget
life's gloomy sorrows in the evening's dark,
upon my lips, a divine melody
recited by a caravan of stars.

How often I have watched stars as they pass
letting the twilight tune my incantations,
and watched the moon bidding the night goodbye,
and roamed the valleys of imagination.
The silence sends a shiver through my spine
beneath the evening's dome, so still and dark,
light dances, painting on my eyelids with
the dreamy palette of a peaceful heart.

لا تَنْشُري الأضـواءَ فـوقَ خميلـتي
إنْ تُشرقي، فلغيرِ قلبي الشاعرِ
مـا عـادَ ضوؤكِ يستثيرُ خـوالجي
حَسبي نجومُ الليلِ تُلهـمُ خاطري
هـنَّ الصديقاتُ السواهرُ في الدُجى
يفهمـنَ روحي وانفجارَ مشاعري
ويُرقِـنَ في جَفني خُيوطَ أشعَّةٍ
فِضيَّةٍ، تحتَ المساءِ الساحرِ

الليلُ ألحـانُ الحيـاة وشِعرُها
ومَطـافُ آلهـةِ الجمـالِ المُلهِمِ
تهفـو عليه النفسُ غير حبيسةٍ
وتحلّــقُ الأرواحُ فـوقَ الأنجُمِ
كم سِـرتُ تحتَ ظَلامـهِ ونجومهِ
فنسِيـتُ أحزانَ الوجـودِ المُظلِمِ
وعـلى في نَغَـمٍ إلهيٍّ الصَدى
تُلقيـهِ قافلةُ النجـومِ عـلى في

كم رُحـتُ أرقـبُ كلَّ نجمٍ عـابرٍ
وأصـوغُ في غَسَقِ الظلامِ ملاحني
أو أرقبُ القَمَـرَ الموِّدَّعَ في الدجى
وأهــيمُ في وادي الخيـالِ الفاتنِ
الصمتُ يبعَثُ في فؤادي رعشةً
تحتَ المسـاءِ المُذهِلِ الساكنِ
والضـوءُ يرقُـصُ في جفوني راسياً
في عُمقِهـا أحـلامُ قلبٍ آمـنِ

And as for you, oh Sun ... what can I say?
What can my feelings hope to find in you?
Don't be surprised that I'm in love with night,
goddess of cruel flames that melt us through.
You rend our dreams on the horizon line,
you decimate what we build in the dark,
you shatter magic visions, ghostly dreams,
and break the silence in a poet's heart.

All of your dancing lights look pale, oh Sun,
compared to my resistance and its fire.
Your mad flames can't tear up my melody
so long as my hands grasp this singing lyre.
And when you flood the earth, remember this:
My temple has no room for your cruel light
I aim to bury the past you revealed
And live beneath the canopy of night.

July 8 1946

يا شمسُ، أمّا أنتِ... ماذا؟ ما الذي
تلقاهُ فيكِ عواطفي وخواطري؟
لا تَعْجَبي إن كنتُ عاشقةَ الدجى
يا ربّة اللّهب المذيب الصاهر
يا مَن تُمَزِّق كلَّ حُلمٍ مُشرقٍ
للحالمينَ وكلَّ طيفٍ ساحرٍ
يا مَن تُهدِّمُ ما يشيّدُهُ الدُجى
والصمتُ في أعماق قلب الشاعر

أضواؤكِ المتراقصاتُ جميعُها
يا شمسُ أضعفُ من لهيب تمرُّدي
وجنونُ ناركِ لن يمزِّقَ نغمتي
ما دام قيثاري المغرِّدُ في يدي
فإذا غمرتِ الأرضَ فَلْتَتَذكّري
أني سأخلي من ضيائكِ مَعبدي
وسأُدفنُ الماضيَ الذي جلّلتِهِ
ليخيِّم الليلُ الجميل على غدي

٨ تموز ١٩٤٦

Elegy for a Drowned Man

The day is gone, river, and evening's here
its silence walks over your gentle waves
the lights on the horizon fade away
making the flock's soft footfalls disappear.

The world has fallen silent, but one wave
still echoes with the myths of bygone times
lamenting its sad fate, it roils and rhymes,
forever giving life's secrets away.

But look there, riverbank! What is this ghost
rising up on that wave, beyond the sand?
Is it a god made young by beauty's hand?
Or a drowned man who lost hold of life's rope?

Tell me, what's floating out there in the dark,
causing disquiet, riverbank, at night?
What is it? I can't see, there is no light,
What is this strange thing troubling my heart?

A skeleton dives, bobs up into view,
submerging, surfacing, in shadows lost
is it a man, I wonder? Or a ghost?
What could it be, darkness? I wish I knew.

مرثية غريق

أيهـا النَهْـرُ لقـد جـاء المسـاءُ
ومَـشَى الصَمْتُ على المـوج الوديعْ
وخبـا في الأفـقِ الخـالي الضيـاءُ
وتَـلاشَى وقْـعُ أقـدامِ القطيـعْ

سكن الكَوْنُ سوى المَوج المُدَوِّي
بأسـاطيرِ العُصـورِ الخَاليـاثْ
لم يَـزَلْ يشكو المقـاديرَ ويَـزْوي
أبـداً للكـونِ أسـرارَ الحيـاةْ

إيـهِ يا ضِفَّـةُ مـا ذاكَ الخيـالُ؟
فـوق صدْرِ الموج، تحـت الظُلماتِ
أإلهٌ قـد تصبَّـاه الجمـالُ؟
أم غريـقٌ عَـزَّهُ حَبْـلُ النجـاةِ؟

حدّثيـني، مـا أرَى خلفَ السِّـياجِ؟
فهـو يا ضِفَّـةُ في الليـلِ مُريـبُ
ما الـذي ألمـح في هذي الـدياجي؟
مـا تـراهُ ذلكَ الشيءُ الغريـبُ؟

هيـكْلٌ يغطُـسُ حينـاً ثمَّ يطفـو
تائهاً تحـتَ دُجى الليـلِ الحزيـنْ
بَـشَرٌ هـذا تـرى؟ أم هـو طيفُ؟
ليتَ شِعْري، يا دياجي، مـا يكونْ؟

11

My poet, look, it is a man who's drowned.
Grieve for this body, tattered and decayed,
supine beneath the dark, he'll never wake,
as light, that sleepless eye, spreads all around.

No loved ones say goodbye as he departs,
he floats alone, exhausted, in the tide.
A stranger is the only one who cried
here on the shore: my melancholy heart.

Winds of the night, be kind to his remains
be still, don't vex the body of the drowned.
The shreds of life are all that he has now,
give him a loyal heart to ease his pain.

And make your waves, soft river, an embrace
receiving him, a sympathetic heart.
Let your light be an eye, o twinkling stars,
shedding radiant tears down the sky's face.

Ah me, my lyre, what fateful tragedies!
Night's lights and shadows fill me up with rancor.
Stop there, you fishermen! Let down your anchors,
watch for his disappearing body, please.

آهِ يا شـاعرتي، هــذا غريـق
فاحزني للجَسَـدِ البـالي المُمَـزَّق
راقـداً، تحـتَ الدياجي، لا يُفيـقُ
والسَّنـا مـن حَـوْلِهِ جَفْـنٌ مؤرَّقُ

يا لَمَيـتٍ لم يودِّعْـهُ قريـبُ
فهـو في النَهـر وحيـدٌ مُتعَـبُ
مـا بكَى مَصْرَعَـهُ إلّا غريـبُ
هـو قلـبي، ذلـكَ المكتئـبُ

يا رياحَ الليـلِ رِفْقـاً بالرَّفـاتِ
واهدأي، لا تُقلقي جسْمَ الغريقِ
حسبُهُ مـا مزَّقـتْ أيـدي الحيـاةِ
فليكُـنْ منـكِ له قلـبُ صديـقِ

ولْتكـنْ، يا نهـرُ، أمواجُكَ حضنا
يتلقَّـاهُ وقلبـاً مُشْفِـقا
ولْتكـنْ، يا نجـمُ، أضـواءُك عينـا
تسكُبُ الدمـعَ علـى مـن غَرِقـا

آهِ يا قيثـارتي، أيُّ المـآسي!
قـد كرِهْـتُ الليـلَ أضـواءً وظـلّا
أيهـا الصيّادُ، قِـفْ! ألـقِ المراسي
إنّ تحـتَ الليـلِ جسْـماً مُضْمَحِلّا

That's it there, fishermen, that is his corpse,
its breath subsiding in the water's arms,
its eyes reflecting terror and alarm,
still filled to brimming with that vital force.

Stop your boats, fishermen, in the low tide
Come fish this man out from waters of pain
Take him to shore, and bury what remains
Of his cold body in the countryside.

Why do you fish in the ocean of time?
Eternity will fish for you tomorrow.
We are, o fishermen, children of sorrow
Eternal sadness lingers in our eyes.

The river's victims pile in days, in years
Tomorrow we'll all drown in the same tide
As death surrounds our world on every side
bringing those in its cruel orbit to tears.

The world is small, fishermen, in my view,
life hides its secrets deep beneath the waves.
When everything we do leads to the grave,
what kind of hopefulness remains to you?

July 10 1945

هـوذا ، يا أيُّهـا الصيّـادُ ، جِسْما
خامـدَ الأنفاسِ في حضْـنِ المياهْ
وعُيــونـاً مُلِئـتْ رَغْبـاً وهَمّـا
لم يَـزَلْ يملأهـا حُـبُّ الحيـاهْ

أيّهـا الصيّـادُ ، قـف بـالـزورقِ ،
وانتَشِـلْ هـذا الغريـقَ البائسـا
خُـذْهُ للشاطئِ وادفِـنْ مـا بَـقِي
منـه في القَرْيـةِ وارجـعْ يائسـا

مـا الـذي تصطـادُ في بحْـرِ الزَمَنْ
وغـداً يصطـادُكَ الدهْـرُ العتِيُّ
نحـن يا صيّـادُ أبنـاءُ الشَّجَـنْ
حفَّ محْيـانا الشَّقَـاءُ الأبـديُّ

كلُّ يـومٍ بــينَ أيدينـا غريـقُ
وغـداً نحـنُ جميعـاً مُغْرَقـونا
عـالَمٌ حفَّ بـه المـوتُ المُحيقُ
وتَبـاكَى في حِمَـاهُ البائسـونا

ضـاقَ يا صيّـادُ في عَيْنـي الوجودُ
يا لَكَـوْنٍ سِـرُّهُ لا يَنْجَـلِي
كلُّ مـا فيـهِ إلى القَـبْرِ يقـودُ
مـا الـذي يَبْقى لنا مـن أَمَلِ؟

١٠ تموز ١٩٤٥

15

Night Lover

You shadows of the night who hide away our hearts' laments,
look now and see this wandering ghost, its face so pale and
    lean
like a strange apparition come to roam beneath your tent,
carrying an oud in its right hand, singing to the unseen,
unbothered by night's stillness in the darkening ravine.

It is a woman, Night. The valley's felt her in its shade.
When dark approached and made her two eyes overflow with
    tears,
she took her songs of suffering and headed to the glade.
If only the songs on her lips, dear Night, could reach your ears,
if only you, Night, could discern her hopes, her dreams, her
    fears.

Seducing her with dark and quiet, nighttime drove her mad.
The silence, with its tempting beauty, made her young again.
She shed the coldness of a day whose path was bleak and sad,
and moved through this unhappy world with longing in her
    heart,
sobs emanating from the oud, sighs pouring from the dark.

You there, woman in love with night and all its lush ravines,
you're nothing but a plaintive sigh when the world's laughter
    rings.
This is the night: divine echoes, visions in blues and greens,
So pick up your oud from the grass, and hold it close, and
    sing,
describe night's art, its beauty, how it enchants everything.

عاشقة الليل

يا ظَـلام الليلِ يا طاوِيَ أحزانِ القلوبِ
أنظُرِ الآنَ فهـذا شَبَحٌ بـادي الشُّحوبِ
جاء يَسْعى ، تحتَ أستارِكَ ، كالطيفِ الغريبِ
حامـلاً في كفِّـه العـودَ يُغـنّي للغيـوبِ
ليس يَغنيهِ سُكونُ الليلِ في الوادي الكئيبِ

هـو ، يا ليـلُ ، فتاةٌ شَهِدَ الـوادي سُـراها
أقبـلَ الليـلُ عليـا فأفاقـتْ مُقلتـاها
ومَضَتْ تستقبلُ الـوادي بألحانٍ أسـاها
ليتَ آفاقَكَ تـدري مـا تُغـنّي شَـفَتاها
آهِ يا ليـلُ ويا ليتَكَ تـدري مـا مُنـاها

جنّهـا الليلُ فأغرتها الدَيَاجي والسكونُ
وتَصَبّاها جمـالُ الصَمتِ ، والصَمتُ فُتونُ
فنَضَتْ بُـردَ نهارٍ لـفّ مَسـراهُ الحنينُ
وسَرَتْ طيفاً حزيناً فـإذا الكونُ حـزينُ
فـمن العـودِ نشـيجٌ ومـن الليـلِ أنـينُ

إيهِ يا عاشـقةَ الليـلِ ووادِيهِ الأغـنّ
هـوذا الليـلُ صَـدَى وحي ورؤيا مُتَمَـنّي
تَضْحكُ الدُنيا وما أنتِ سِوى آهةِ حُزْنِ
تُخْـذي العودَ عن العُشـبِ وضُمّيه وغـني
وصِفي مـا في المساءِ الحُلوِ مـن سِحْرٍ وفنّ

17

What in the sky enchants us, poet of perplexity?
Is it our youthful dreams, our poetic imagination?
Is it our love of the unknown? A night of misery?
Or is it the enchanted lights dancing on the horizon?
How strange, lyre of the evening, poet of tranquility.

Your specter wanders through a cloud, pale-colored and
    sublime,
ever-exploring visions wrapped in an expanse of night.
They're secrets, shadow-lover, overrunning their confines.
But mercy's scarce for broken hearts, my poet; you should go.
Don't ask the lightning for advice, what does its flashing know?

Strange, poet of perplexity – what has distracted you?
Why do you stand there dreaming like a ghost beneath the palms,
holding your head between your hands, with darkness all around,
as though in thought, in sadness, and in silence you had drowned,
not knowing dark's temptation hides there, crouching, in the calm.

Listen – these are the storms, this is the thunder, hear it peal.
Turn back – you will not understand, no matter how you seek
We'll never know what mysteries the folds of life conceal.
My girl, the storm knows nothing, though it rages, raves and
    shrieks,
Have mercy on your heart, for these shadows will never speak.

April 4 1945

ما الذي، شاعرةَ الحَيْرةِ، يُغري بالمساءِ؟
أهي أحـلامُ الصَبـايا أم خيـالُ الشـعراءِ؟
أم هـو الإغـرامُ بالمجهولِ أم ليـلُ الشقاءِ؟
أم تـرى الآفاقُ تَستهويكِ أم سِحْرُ الضياءِ؟
عجبـاً شـاعرةَ الصمتِ وقيثـارَ المساءِ

طيفُكِ الساري شحوبٌ وجلالٌ وغموضُ
لم يـزَل يَسْري خيالاً لأنّه الليلُ العريضُ
فهـو يا عاشـقةَ الظُلْمـةِ أسـرارٌ تَفيضُ
آه يا شـاعرتي لـن يـرْحَمَ القلبُ المَهيضُ
فارجعي لا تسألي البَرْق فـا يدري الوميضُ

عجبـاً، شاعرةَ الحَيْرةِ، مـا سـرُّ الذُهولِ؟
ما الذي ساقكِ طيفاً حالماً تحتَ النخيلِ؟
مُسنَدَ الرأسِ إلى الكفَّينِ في الظلِّ الظليلِ
مُغْرَقاً في الفكرِ والأحزانِ والصمتِ الطويلِ
ذاهلاً عن فتنةِ الظُلْمـةِ في الحقلِ الجميلِ

أنْصتي هذا صُراخُ الرعدِ، هذي العاصفاتُ
فارجـعي لـن تُدْركي سرّاً طوتْه الكائنـاتُ
قـد جَهِلْنـاه وضنّتْ بخفاياهُ الحيـاةُ
ليس يَدْري العاصفُ المجنونُ شيئاً يا فتاةُ
فارحمي قلبَكِ، لن تَنْطقَ هذي الظُلُماتُ

٤ نيسان ١٩٤٥

To the Poet Keats

AFTER HIS POEM "ODE TO A NIGHTINGALE"

My life, the pains of my most solemn soul,
    my bitter dreams all wilting on the vine,
and the procession of my fleeting days,
    and the grim specters of a future time,
all gathered into a bouquet of scents
    which kept my passing spirit in its hold.
I gave the bouquet, like a dreamy song,
    to your unchained and everlasting soul.

My life, poet of mine, is nothing more
    than that of a pensive and dreamy daughter:
her spirit is divine, but here on Earth,
    she is but a handful of clay and water.
Tortured by screams of sorrow ringing out,
    shivering with the shocks of many years,
if not for you, she would not view the grave
    as solace; she would not be drawn to tears.

إلى الشاعر كيتس

الإشارات إلى قصيدته "ODE TO A NIGHTINGALE"

حيـاتي وآلامُ روحي الحـزينْ
وأحـلامي المُـرّةُ الذاويـه
وموكبُ أيّـامَي الذاهبـاتِ
وأطيـافُ أيّـامي الآتيـه

تَجَمَّعْـنَ في باقـةٍ مـن عبيـر
ثَـوَتْ خلفهـا روحيَ الفانيـه
وأهديتُهـا نَغَمـاً حالمـاً
إلى روحِكَ الحُـرّةِ الباقيـه

حيـاتي، يا شـاعري، كلُّهـا
حيـاةُ فتـاةٍ مـن الحالمِيـنْ
إلهيّـةُ الـروح لكنّهـا
علـى الأرضِ حَفنـةُ مـاءٍ وطـينْ
تُعذِّبهـا صَرخـات الأسـى
وتُرْوِعُشهـا صَدَمـاتُ السنِيـنْ
ولـولاكَ مـا وجـدتْ في الثَّرى
عـزاءً ولم يَجْتذِبهـا الحنِيـنْ

Your sweet, eternal, and melodic odes
    are my odes too; I sing them in my voice.
I've called on them so many winter nights
    to drive away the storm's loud, raucous noise.
I've sung them to the fire in my hearth
    and felt them waking fiery temptation,
I've sung them to night's shadows, stretched out wide
    and felt them stir overflowing sensation.

I've stood next to the river many nights
    in melancholy autumn, listening
for the voice of a gentle nightingale
    who, perched upon the branches, softly sings.
I search for your sad strains inside its voice,
    for your complaints between thinking and pain,
I ask it about youth and how it fades,
    the shadow of a young man in his grave.

I ask the nightingale to paint again
    the distant darkness of a gloomy night
enfolding my poet, or what remained
    of him: destructive grief and moans of fright.
Describe the sadness on the sick man's face,
    his loneliness, his pleading, scattered cries
describe his body and the things he said
    when he lay down and bid the world goodbye.

أناشـيـدُكَ الخالـداتُ العِـذاب
نشـــيدي وأغنيـــتي الهاتفــه
فـكم ليـلةٍ مـن ليـالي الشتـاء
دفعـــتُ بهـا ضَجَّـةَ العاصفـه
وأسمعتُهـــا النـــارَ في مَوْقِدي
وغنّيتُهـــا الظُـــلّةَ الوارفــه
وأيقظـــتُ في ظلّهـا فِتْنتـي
ونـــارَ عواطـفي الجارفــه

وكم في ليـالي الخريـفِ الكئيـب
وقفـــتُ أحـدّقُ عنـد النَّهَـر
أصيـــخُ إلى صـوتِ قُمْرِيَّـةٍ
سَجَحتْ فوقَ بعضِ غُصونِ الشَّجَر
أفتـشُ في صَوْتِهـا عـن شَجـاكَ
وشـكواكَ بـين الأسى والفِكَـر
وأسـألُها عـن شَـبابٍ ذَوَى
وظـلِّ صِبـاً راقـدٍ في الحَفَـر

أقـولُ لهـا: صَـوِّري مـن جديـد
ظـلامَ المسـاءِ الكئيـبِ البعيـذ
ومـا كانَ مـن شـاعري في دُجَـاه
وآهاتِـــه وأسَـاهُ المُبيـذ
صِـفي حُزْنَـهُ عنـد رأسِ المريض
ووحشـتَهُ والرَّحَـاءَ البَديـذ
صِـفي ذلـك الجَسَـدَ الآدمـيَّ
ومـا قـالَ عنـدَ وَدَاعِ الوُجـوذ

Describe, my poet, how the evening passed
    stretching cold fingers up the dead man's feet,
tilting its head to hear the tender songs,
    listening carefully to every beat.
Describe the way his short life made him shake
    with grief, beneath the unsheathed sword of death,
his poet's head enclosed in his two hands,
    alone beside the corpse, awake, bereft.

How did the forlorn evening take control
    over the fading candle's dying flame?
Did tempests shriek and bellow in the dark?
    What did his roaring, dying soul exclaim?
"Where youth grows pale, and specter-thin, and dies;
    Where but to think is to be full of sorrow ... "
Where this strange numbness finally says goodbye
    to the desires' spirits as they go.

The nights march on and on into their graves
    and life follows behind in the procession
I too walk through the caverns of the world,
    searching for tired dreams, weak aspirations.
The nightingales deceive me as I pass,
    taunting and teasing, warbling in quartets,
while your ghost hides away in secrecy,
    veiled in the violet shadow of sunset.

February 6 1947

صِفِي شاعري كيف أمضى المساء
على قَدَمَي ذلكَ المَيِّتِ
يُصيخُ إلى النَغَماتِ الحَنون
ويُطرقُ إطراقةَ المُنصِتِ
صفيهِ، كما أرعشتُهُ الحياة
أسئ، تحتَ سيف الرَدى المُضلِّتِ
على كفِّهِ رأسُهُ الشاعريُّ
وحيداً، إلى جانبِ الجِثَّةِ

وكيفَ توَلّى المساءُ الحزين
على شُعْلةِ الشمعةِ الشاحبه؟
وهل صَرَخَتْ في الظلام الرياح
كما صَرَخَتْ نفسُهُ الصاخبه؟
"هنالكَ حيثُ يموتُ الشباب
وتَذْوي أشِعَّتُهُ الغاربه"
هنالكَ حيثُ الذهولُ الغريب
يوَدِّعُ روحَ المُنى الذاهبه

وتَمْضي الليالي إلى قَبْرِها
وتَمْشي الحياةُ معَ الموكبِ
أسيرُ أنا في شِعابِ الوجود
أُفَتِّشُ عن حُلُمي المُتْعَبِ
تُخَادعُني كلُّ قمرِيَّةٍ
وتعبَثُ كلُّ الأغاريدِ بي
وما زالَ طيفُكَ طيَّ الخَفاء
تُحَجِّبُهُ ظُلمةُ المَغْرِبِ

٦ شباط ١٩٤٧

POEMS FROM
SHRAPNEL AND ASH
(1949)

قصائد من
شظايا ورمـاد
(١٩٤٩)

The Train Passed By

Night's stillness stretches out into the distance
broken only by doves who, from afar,
coo on, confused, and dogs who bark at ancient stars
as hungry clocks devour our existence.
Out there, in one direction or another
the train passed by
wheels spinning, pleading. I have spent the night
waiting for it and day to come. The train
passed by then disappeared into the dark
behind the far-off hills
a feeble echo in my heart
as I stare at the dreaming stars
imagining the wheels and rows
of tired, sleepless passengers,
imagining the weight of night
on eyelids sick of others' faces
flickering in faded light,
and silent shadows. I can see
the bitter irritation
in souls that grow more worn with every station,
their luggage waiting, as they must,
like luggage, wait beneath a layer of dust
sleeping a moment, woken by the train
some of them yawning, sleeping, peering out
into the wastelands speeding by

مر القطار

الليلُ ممتدُّ السكونِ إلى المَدَى
لا شيءَ يقطعُهُ سوى صوتٍ بليدْ
لحمامةٍ حَيْرى وكلبٍ ينبَحُ النجمَ البعيذْ
والساعةُ البلهاءُ تلتهم الغدا
وهناك في بعضِ الجهاتْ
مرَّ القطارْ

عجلاتُهُ غزلتْ رجاءً بتُّ أنتظرُ النهارْ
من أجلهِ... مرَّ القطارْ
وخبا بعيداً في السكونْ
خلفَ التلالِ النائياتْ

لم يبقَ في نفسي سوى رجْعٍ وَهُونْ
وأنا أحدّقُ في النجومِ الحَالماتْ
أتخيّلُ العرباتِ والصفَّ الطويلْ
من ساهرينَ ومتعبينْ
أتخيلُ الليلَ الثقيلْ

في أعينٍ سئمتْ وجوهَ الراكبينْ
في ضوءِ مصباحِ القطارِ الباهتِ
سئمتْ مراقبةَ الظلامِ الصامتِ
أتصوّرُ الضجَرَ المريرْ
في أنفسٍ ملّتْ وأتعبها الصفيرْ

هي والحقائبُ في انتظارْ
هي والحقائبُ تحت أكداسِ الغبارْ
تغفو دقائقَ ثم يوقظُها القطارْ
ويُطلُّ بعضُ الراكبينْ
متثائباً، نعسانَ، في كسلٍ يحدّق في القِفارْ

29

then into others' weary eyes
faces of strangers gathered by a train.
Almost asleep, they dimly hear
a cranky mumbling in one ear
"My watch is slow! How long has passed?
and when do we arrive?"
His watch chimes three o'clock indifferently
and here the whistle cuts him off
the train conductor's lantern glows,
and through the night, the station lights
appear, the weary train begins to slow.
One young man sits apart
refusing sleep but sighing still,
awake, surveying stars, his eyes
are edged with worry, cold, his face
red-hued from fever-dreams, his lips
almost apart reveal a dream
imbuing night with rustlings
the quiet melody of wings,
his two eyes almost closed as though
afraid a ray might pierce the lids
revealing some intolerable thing.
This anxious, sad young man
tries everything he can to see
something besides the ancient mystery

ويعودُ ينظُرُ في وجوهِ الآخرينْ

في أوجهِ الغُرباء يجمعُهم قطارْ

ويكادُ يغفو ثم يسمَعُ في شُرُودْ

صوتاً يغمغمُ في بُرُودْ

"هذي العقاربُ لا تسيرْ!

كم مرَّ من هذا المساء؟ متى الوصولُ؟"

وتدقُّ ساعتُهُ ثلاثاً في ذُهُولْ

وهنا يقاطعُهُ الصفيرْ

ويلوحُ مصباحُ الخفيرْ

ويلوحُ ضوءُ محطةٍ عَبْرَ المساء

إذ ذاكَ يتَّئدُ القطارُ المُجهَدُ

... وفتىً هنالكَ في انطواءْ

يأبَى الرقادَ ولم يزلْ يتنهدُ

سهرانَ يرتقبُ النجومْ

في مقلتيه برودةٌ خطَّ الوجومْ

أطرافَها... في وجههِ لونٌ غريبْ

ألقتْ عليه حرارةُ الأحلامِ آثارَ احمرازْ

شَفتاهُ في شبهِ افترازْ

عن شبهِ حُلمٍ يفرِّشُ الليلَ الجديبْ

يحفيفِ أجنحةٍ خفيّاتِ اللُحونْ

عيناه في شِبهِ انطباقْ

وكأنّها تخشَى فرارَ أشعةٍ خلف الجفونْ

أو أن ترى شيئاً مقيتاً لا يُطَاقْ

هذا الفتى الضَجِرُ الحزينْ

عبثاً يحاول أن يَرى في الآخرينْ

شيئاً سوى اللُغزِ القديمْ

the epic story with a thousand parts
its heroes and its language worn and cold
repeating endlessly.
This boy –
               now footsteps pass
a frowning face
peers through the glass
the lamp swings in his hand, he sees
faces exhausted, sleeping sitting up
inside the train
expectant eyes
a desperate cry for dawn in every lid
as the conductor's footsteps fade
into the shadows, stagnant, still.

The train passed through a wasteland and was gone
I stood alone, asking the night
when it would bring my poet back
which train will bring him back to me?
Did the conductor wander through his car
passing his lamp over the passengers
seeing them without seeing, moving on
while I remain here,
waiting for the train?

1948

والقصةِ الكبرى التي سئِمَ الوجودْ
أبطالَها وفصولَها ومضَى يراقبُ في برودْ
تَكُرارَها البالي السقيمْ
هذا الفتى ...
وتمرُّ أقدامُ الخفيرْ
ويُطلُّ وجهٌ عابسٌ خلفَ الزُّجاجِ ،
وجهُ الخفيرْ!
ويهزُّ في يدِهِ السراجَ
فيرى الوجوهَ المتعَبه
والنائمينَ وهُم جلوسٌ في القطارْ
والأعينَ المترقبه
في كلِّ جَفْنٍ صرخةٌ باسمِ النهارْ ،
وتضيعُ أقدامُ الخفير الساهِر
خلفَ الظلام الراكِدِ

مرَّ القطارُ وضاع في قلبِ القفارْ
وبقيت وحدي أسألُ الليلَ الشَّرودْ
عن شاعري ومتى يعودْ ؟
ومتى يجيءُ به القطارْ ؟
أتراهُ مرَّ به الخفيرْ
وراَه لم يعبأ به... كالآخرينْ
ومضى يسيرْ
هو والسراجُ ويفحصانِ الراكبينْ
وأنا هنا ما زلتُ في انتظارْ
وأوَدُّ لو جاءَ القطارُ ...

١٩٤٨

Elegy for an Unimportant Day

I watched as darkness fell on distant skies
bringing an end to this uncanny day
I heard its echoes as they passed away
into the caverns of my memory
Tomorrow life goes back to how it was
a thirsty lip and cup
whose depths reflect
colored with wine
but when I bring my lips
to touch its edge
they taste no trace of memory's sweetness
they taste no trace.

I watched this strange day tumble to its end
and at its end, even my sins
and the stupidities
I call my memories
even they wept
and now there's nothing in my hands
but the remembrance of a song
screaming inside
mourning the way my hand let go of life
of memory, of youthful days
mourning the way
everything fell, as if into mirage,
lost in the fog.

I lost another day of life
and cast it willingly onto
the pile of remnants from my youth

مرثية يوم تافه

لاحتِ الظلمةُ في الأُفق السحيقِ
وانتهى اليومُ الغريبُ
ومضت أصداؤه نحو كهوفِ الذكرياتِ
وغداً تمضي كما كانت حياتي
شفةٌ ظمأى وكوبُ
عكست أعماقُه لونَ الرحيقِ
وإذا ما لمستهُ شفتايا
لم تجدْ من لذّةِ الذكرى بقايا
لم تجد حتى بقايا

انتهى اليومُ الغريبُ
انتهى وانتحبتُ حتى الذنوبُ
وبكت حتى حماقاتي التي سمّيتُها
ذكرياتي
انتهى لم يبقَ في كفّيِ منه
غيرُ ذكرى نَغَمٍ يصرخُ في أعماق ذاتي
راثياً كفّي التي أفرغتُها
من حياتي ، واذّكاراتي ، ويومٍ من شبابي
ضاعَ في وادي السرابِ
في الضبابِ .

كان يوماً من حياتي
ضائعاً ألقيتُه دون اضطرابِ
فوق أشلاء شبابي

a hill of thoughts
thousands of hours lost
in fog
in labyrinths of night.

It was an unimportant day, and strange
the way the lazy clock counted the seconds off
It wasn't a day of my life
it was, rather, the frightening realization
of memory's curse I tattered
the glass that I once shattered
over a grave of buried hopes
behind the years
behind myself.

It was an unimportant day, till night
the hours passed half-crying tears
till night
when his sweet voice stirred in my ears
sweet voice I thought I'd lost
till dark engulfed the sky
and every trace of pain
was wiped away
even my sins
my lover's voice
was wiped away
the hands of dusk
carried its echoes to a place
my heart can't see
leaving only love's memory
the echo of an unimportant day
begging to hear my lover's voice in vain.

1948

عند تلِّ الذكرياتِ
فوق آلافٍ من الساعاتِ تاهت في الضَبابِ
في مَتاهاتِ الليالي الغابِراتِ

كان يوماً تافهاً. كان غريبا
أن تَدُقَّ الساعةُ الكَسلى وتُحصي لَحَظاتي
إنه لم يكُ يوماً من حياتي
إنه قد كان تحقيقاً رهيبا
لبقايا لعنةِ الذكرى التي مزّقتُها.
هي والكأسُ التي حطَّمتها
عند قبرِ الأملِ المَيِّت ، خلفَ السنواتِ ،
خلف ذاتي

كان يوماً تافهاً... حتى المساءِ
مرت الساعاتُ في شِبهِ بكاءٍ
كلُّها حتى المساءِ
عندما أيقظَ سمعي صوتُه
صوتُه الحُلوُ الذي ضيَّعتُه
عندما أحدقتِ الظلمةُ بالأفقِ الرهيبِ
وامتحى صوتُ حبيبي
حملت أصداءه كفُّ الغروبِ
لمكانٍ غابَ عن أعينِ قلبي
غابَ لم تبقَ سوى الذكرى وحتى
وصدى يومٍ غريبٍ
كشحوبي
عبثاً أُضرَعُ أن يُرجِعَ لي صوتَ حبيبي.

١٩٤٨

At the End of the Stairs

Days pass, smothered
We haven't met
not even in the ghost of a mirage
I am alone, surviving on the sound
of shadows' feet
behind the pane
behind the door
I am alone
          days pass
crawling and cold
dragging my discontent and doubt
I listen
counting anxious minutes
has time passed?
or is this timelessness?
Days pass
heavy with longing
Where am I?
still staring at the stairs
I see their base
but cannot see the end
I see their base but cannot see
the door.

Days pass
We haven't met, you're there
beyond the sprawling of my dreams
horizons wrapped in mystery
I walk, I see, I sleep

نهاية السُّلَّم

مرّت أيامٌ منطفئاتْ
لم نلتقِ لم يجمعْنا حتى طيفُ سَرابْ
وأنا وحدي، أقتاتُ بوقْعِ خُطى الظُّلماتْ
خلف زُجاج النافذةِ الفظّةِ، خلفَ البابْ
وأنا وحدي...

مرَّت أيَّامْ
باردةً تزحفُ ساحبةً ضَجَري المرتابْ
وأنا أُصغي وأعُدُّ دقائقَها القلقاتْ
هل مرَّ بنا زمنٌ؟ أم خُضنا اللازمنا؟
مرّت أيام
أيامٌ تُثقلُها أشواقي. أينَ أنا؟
ما زلتُ أُحدِّقُ في السُّلَّم
والسُّلمُ يبدأُ لكنْ أينَ نهايتُه؟
يبدأُ. أين البابُ المبهَمْ؟
بابُ السُّلَّمْ؟

مرّت أيام
لم نلتقِ، أنتَ هناك وراءَ مَدَى الأحلامْ
في أفقٍ حفَّ به المجهول وأنا أمشي، وأرى، وأنامْ

use up my days
as every sweet tomorrow flees
into the wasted past.
My time, consumed by sighs –
when are you back?
Days pass, and you forget
about the love you left behind
in a lost corner of your heart
pleading, crying, and torn apart,
please give me light.

Come back. To meet
would give us wings
to cross the night
there is a sky
behind the forest, there are seas
unbounded, seething, waves
made from the foam of dreams and churned
by hands of light.

Come back, or else my voice
will die behind some crooked turn
inside your ear
and I'll be here
cast out into forgetting's core
nothing but silence canopied
over my sadness, nothing more
sleep's echo whispering
inside my ear, he won't be back
he won't be back.

1948

أستنفدُ أيامي وأجرُ غدي المعسولُ
فيفرُ إلى الماضي المفقودْ
أيامي تأكلُها الآهات متى ستعودْ؟
مرّتْ أيامٌ لم تتذكرْ أن هناكَ
في زاويةٍ من قلبكَ حُباً مهجورا
عضّتُ في قدَمَيهِ الأشواكُ
حباً يتضرّعُ مذعورا
هَبه النورا

عُدْ. بعضَ لقاءٍ
يمنحُنا أجنحةً نجتازُ الليلَ بها
فهناكَ فضاءٌ
خلفَ الغاباتِ الملتفّاتِ، هناكَ بحورٌ
لا حدَّ لها تُرغي وتموزُ
أمواجٌ من زَبَد الأحلام تقلِّبُها
أيدٍ من نورْ

عدْ، أم سيموتُ
صوتي في سمعكَ خلف المُنعرَج الممقوتْ
وأظلُّ أنا شاردةً في قلب النسيانْ
لا شيءَ سوى الصمتِ الممدودْ
فوقَ الأحزانْ لا شيءَ سوى رجْعِ نعسانْ
يهمِسُ في سمعي ليس يعودْ
لا ليس يعودْ

١٩٤٨

41

Song of the Abyss

I hate the twisting corridors
of souls
of shining eyes
I hate the stillness too
and all the thoughts that hide
inside a glass
the thought of echo and of rage
the thought of misdeeds shining
bright as stars
their touch a burning flame
the color of torment.
I hate the captivating eyes
behind whose smiling skies
there burns the flame of hate.
I hate the trembling hands
behind whose warm embrace
there lurks a hardness like
the insignificance of life
to corpses lying in their graves
ravaged by worms.
I hate the echo of a prayer
trembling on a sinful lip,
in every word a crime
where base desires roil. I hate
my never-ending quest for good
for love, for my ideals.

أغنية الهاوية

مجحتُ الزوايا التي تلتوي
وراءَ النفوسْ
وراءَ بريقِ العُيونْ
وأبغضتُ حتى السُكونْ
وتلكَ المعاني التي تنطوي
عليها الكؤوسْ

معاني الصَدَى والجُنونْ
معاني الخطايا التي تُبرِقُ
بريقَ النجومْ
وفي لمسها اللهبُ المُحرقُ
ولونُ الهمومْ
كرهتُ الجفونَ التي تأسُرُ
وخلفَ سماءِ ابتساماتها
لهيبِ الحقود
كرهتُ الأكفَّ التي تعصرُ
وخلفَ حرارةٍ رَعشاتها
جمودٌ كذُلِّ الحياه
على جُثةٍ تحت بعض اللحودْ
تعيثُ بها دودةٌ في برودْ
كرهتُ ارتعاشَ الشفاهْ
برَجعِ الصلاه
ففي كُلِّ لفظٍ خطيئه
تجيشُ بها رَغباتٌ دنيئه
وعفتُ طُموحي وبحثي الطويلْ
عن الخيرِ، والحبِّ، والمُثلِ العاليه

43

I hate having aspired to
an impossible world
behind this ruse
the chasm lurks.
I hate my madness, old and new
I'll send it someplace far away
where I'll bury desire too
and call it heaven for delusionals.
The years will pass
why do I feel this pain
these hands of rain
wrapping a noose of thought
around my neck?
Where can I go with this unceasing heart
still here, not growing cold
or burning up,
a sphinx's heart. What next?
I feel my life dissolving
Wait one second
hold your frigid hand
the song of the abyss
is calling to my roving feet
and laying out a path
I ask life's noose to wait one second
please don't leave me hanging here
over the air
my recent past has disappeared
behind the bend

وحقّرتُ سعيي إلى عالمٍ مستحيلْ

فخلفَ انخداعي تنتظرُ الهاويه

وعفتُ جنوني القديمَ وعفتُ الجديدْ

وأودعتهُ في مكانٍ بعيدْ

دفنتُ به رَغَباتِ البشرْ

وسمّيتهُ جنة الواهمين

ستمضي السنينْ

لماذا أُحسُّ الأسى والضَّجَرْ

وكفُّ المطَرْ

تلفُّ على عنقي المختنقْ

حبالَ الفِكَرْ؟

وأينَ أسيرُ وقلبي النزقْ

هنالكَ ما زالَ ، لا يبرُدُ

ولا يحترقْ

كقلبِ أبي الهول . أين الغدُ؟

أُحسُّ حياتي تذوبْ

ففي لحظةً واحده

ولا تَسحبي يَدكِ البارده

فأغنيةُ الهاويه

تُهيبُ بأقدامي الشارده

وتَلوي الدروبْ

ففي لحظةً يا حبالَ الحياه

ولا تتركيني هنا

معلقةً بالفراغِ الرهيبْ

فأمسي القريبْ

تلاشى على آخرِ المنحنى

the shadow of tomorrow's hope
will hide its sighs if I relent.
Wait just one second
stop your frigid hand
the song of the abyss
plays on criminal lips
repeating madly in my ears
repeating, I can no longer be still
I almost march to the abyss
with others, marching, burying
the remnants of
tomorrow's dreams
forgetting all.

1948

وظلُّ غدي
تَلثَّم أواهُ لو أهتدي.
قفي لحظةً واحده
ولا تَسحبي يَدَكِ البارده
فأغنيةُ الهاويه
تردّدها الأنفسُ الجانيه
تكثّرها في جُنونْ
على سمعي المُجهَدِ
تكثّرُها لم يَعُدْ لي سكونْ
أكادُ أسيرُ إلى الهاويه
مـع السائريْن
وأدفِنُ آخرَ أحلاميه
وأنسى غدي

١٩٤٨

To My Late Aunt

I stare into the sky at dawn, silent and powerless
as memories echo, whisper, and tremble on my lips.
A dead and distant past lives on inside this seething wound,
its days the echo of a dream of which nothing remains
but fragments, shreds of smiles weighed down with sickness
     and with pain.

Memories come in waves, filling my heart with mournful
     ghosts
the melancholy of the past, still warm, reminding me
of what has been: nights steeped in blood, dawn racked with
     burning thirst,
tears pouring, searing, sadness washing over me in floods,
inundations of cold despair, resisting flame and fire.

What dreams lie in the past? What cures for this feverish pain?
Echoes of whispered memories? A plea saved from the flames?
A passing phrase? A smile? Soft hands to smooth over my
     fear?
I want a refuge from my sorrows and my sleepless nights,
some of your smile as it goes down, setting the sky alight.

I shed a tear, the tear sheds me, heart dying, mad with hurt
droplets of fire in my bloodstream, tearing me apart.
Eyes burn with pain and bleed, oozing, shedding old images
They seem like wounds, not eyes, seeking tomorrow's
     radiance.
Why do life's sunbeams shine at night, while fate muddies
     the air?

إلى عمَّتي الراحلة

أنا لم أزل في الفجر رانيــــة   للأفـــق في صمتٍ وإعياءِ
تتدافـــعُ الذكرى على شفتي   بعضَ ارتعاشاتٍ وأصداءِ
الجُرحُ نديانٌ تعيشُ بـه   أصداءُ ماضٍ ميّتٍ ناءِ
أيامـــهُ عادت صَدَى حلمٍ   لم تَبقَ منه غيرُ أشلاءِ
غيرُ ابتساماتٍ ممزّقةٍ   أودثُ بهنّ مرارةَ الداءِ

تتدافـــعُ الذكرى وتملأني   أشباحها قلقاً وأشجــانا
الأمـــسُ ما زالـت كآبته   حرّى تذكِّرني بمــا كانا:
بالليــل كيفَ سهرتـه ألمـاً   بالفجر كيفَ أطلَّ ظمآنا
بدمـــوعي العطشى وحرقتها   بتدفـق الإحساس أحزانا
باليأس كيف طغت مرارته   وتمـــرّدت حُرقاً ونيرانا

الأمسُ هل في الأمس من حُلمٍ   هل فيه ما يُنجي من الحَرقِ؟
هل فيه بعضُ صدى يناغمني   ذكرىً؟ رجاءٌ غيرُ محترق
لفظٌ يمرُّ؟ وبسمةٌ ويدٌ   مرّت برقّتها على قَلَتي؟
أوّاه. بعض خطى ألوذ بها   من حزني القاسي ومن أرقي
بعض ابتسامتك التي غربت   في الصمت واحترقت على الأفق

الدمـــعُ أذرفـهُ ويذرفني   قلبـاً يحنُّ أسىً ويُحتضَرُ
قطراتـهُ نارٌ تمزّقـني   ما زال منها في دمي أثـرُ
عينـايَ تحترقـان من ألمٍ   تدمى وتقطرُ فيهما الصور
جرحانِ لا جفنان أين غدي؟   أين الطبيعة والهوى النضرُ؟
مـا للحيـاةِ هَوَت أشعتُها   ليلاً وعكر جوُّها القدرُ؟

49

Cruel images block off my path no matter where I turn
my bloodshot eyes seal shut with memories that shatter me.
Why was it you who died, while I live with these fantasies,
while I live through this tattered life, weaving my dreams with
    love,
feeling thirst cast a pall on me when my thoughts turn to you?

Shuddering, sleepless sadness strangles me. Let me forget
the wound you etched with worry in my dreams and poetry.
I miss the feeling of your soft hand passing through my hair,
all that remains now is the bitter song I sing and sing
in nights held captive by the dawn, dry crust upon my lips.

My sadness and my thirst – have you become a dead-eyed
    ghost?
Have you traded my trembling heart's arms for the grave's
    embrace?
No bird can stir love in your veins now, nothing resurrect
dead hopes. When shadows passed, you did not feel their
    drunken dance,
when timid stars appeared, you paid no mind, rigid and still.

Life's echoes pass over your pillow – the muezzin's voice
you once stayed up to hear now rests forever in your ears.
Why must it resonate inside a heart that has forgotten
how to beat? Why shelter in this exile, making Najaf weep?
The city shudders, crying through the night, renouncing sleep.

أين التفتُّ تصدُّني صوَرٌ وحشيةٌ، وشتيتُ آلام
ذكرئ مـن المـاضي تحطمُني وتظل تصهرُ جفنّي الدامي
أوّاه. كيـفَ سقطتِ ميتـةً وأنا أعيشُ وتلك أوهـامي
وأنا أعيـشُ رؤئ ممزّقـةً وأحوكُ أهـوائي وأحلامي
تتلفّـتُ الذكرى إليكِ وبي ظمـأً يعتّم جوَّ أيـامي

وأريـدُ أن أنسى فتخنقُني رَعَشاتُ حُـزنٍ ساهدٍ مُـرَّ
أبقيتِ جُرحـاً حافراً قلقاً في قلبِ أحلامي وفي شِـعري
كفُّ الحنانِ نسيتُ ملمسَها وفقدت معبَرَها على شَعري
لم يبـقَ منهـا غيـرَ أغنيـةٍ جفّت مرارتُها على ثَغري
وسهـرتُ أنشدها وأنشـدها في ليلةٍ مأسورةِ الفَجرِ

أواهُ مـن حُـزني ومن ظمـأي هل عـدت طيفاً مطفأ المُقَلِ
القبرُ ضمَّـكِ في برودتـه بعد ارتعاشـةِ قلبي الخَضلِ
لا طيـرَ يوقظُ فيكِ عِـرْقَ هـوىً لا شيءَ يبعثُ خامدَ الأملِ
الظلُّ مـرَّ وأنتِ ساهيةٌ عـن رَقْصِـهِ وشُـعاعِه الثمِلِ
والنجمُ لاحَ وأنتِ هامدةٌ لا تعبـأين بضوئـه الخَجِلِ

وتمـرُّ أصداءُ الحيـاةِ ضُحًى بوسـادِكِ المحـزونِ وأسَـفا
صوتُ المـؤذّنِ كم سهرتِ له مـا بالُه في مسمعيكِ غَـفا؟
مـا بـالُ رعشتِه تمـرُّ على قلب تناسى كيف أمسِ هَفا
مـا بالهـا لاذث بغُربتها ومضتْ تُبـاكي حولكِ (النجفا)
تبـكي وترسِـم في انتفاضتها صوتاً يبيّتُ الليلَ مُرتجبـا

Do you feel lonely in the grave when I caress your bed?
Stray strands of hair set fire to my screaming, sick despair,
the hollow in your pillow: fallen planet in my heart,
did your withering body leave some warmth inside this shirt?
No mangled hand can end your life – it lives on in my tears.

I hear my own voice shaking, can you hear its echoes too?
Why must I wake while you stay stiff, gripped in talons of
    pain,
songs stumble, jostle moans of hurt for space upon my lips,
I've ripped to shreds what came before, I've buried joys to
    come,
laughter is futile now, I let happiness die with you.

1948

أوحيـدةٌ في القَـبْرِ هامـدةٌ   وأنـا أَمَــسُّ سريـرَكِ الخـاوي؟

خُصَـلاتُ شعركِ فوقهُ حـرَقٌ في   عُمْـقِ يأسِي الصارخ الـداوي

ومكانُ رأِسكِ في الوسادةِ في   قلـبي بقـايا كوكـبٍ هـاو

وقميصُـكِ البـاكي أمـا بقيـتْ   فيه حرارةُ جسـمِكِ الـذاوي؟

كيـف انطويتِ وأنتِ خالـدةٌ في   أدمـي؟ شُـلَّتْ يـدُ الطاوي

أصْـغي وهل تُصْغِين؟ هل بَلَغَتْ   مشـواكِ أصـداءُ ارتعاشـاتي

كيـف انتفضتُ وأنـتِ هامـدةٌ في   مُخلَّـبَيْ ألمي وآهـــاتي

تتعـثَّرُ النَغَمـاتُ في شـفتي   بــصُراخ أحـزاني وأنّــاتي

مزّقـتُ أيامي الـتي سَـلفَتْ   ودفنـتُ فيـكِ بشاشـةَ الآتي

وأضعـتُ أفـراحي ومـن عَبَـثٍ   شِـبْهُ ابتسـاماتي وضُحْـكاتي

١٩٤٨

Cholera

in the night
listen to echoed moans as they fall
in the depths of the dark, in the still, on the dead
voices rise, voices clash
sadness flows, catches fire
echoed sighs, stuttered cries
every heart boils with heat
silent hut wracked with sobs
spirits scream through the dark everywhere
voices weep everywhere
this is what death has done
they are dead, they are dead, they are dead
let the screaming Nile cry over what death has done

in the dawn
listen to passing feet as they fall
in the still of the dawn, watch and hear the procession of tears
ten are dead, twenty dead
countless dead, hear the tears
hear the pitiful child
they are dead, many lost
they are dead, there is no future left
bodies strewn everywhere, everywhere the bereaved
not a moment to mourn, not a pause
this is death's handiwork

الكوليرا

سكَنَ الليلُ
أصغِ إلى وَقعِ صَدَى الأنّاتْ
في عُمْقِ الظلمةِ ، تحتَ الصمتِ ، على الأمواتْ
صَرَخاتٌ تعلو ، تضطربُ
حزنٌ يتدفّقُ ، يلتهبُ
يتعثّرُ فيه صَدَى الآهاتْ
في كل فؤادٍ غليانُ
في الكوخِ الساكنِ أحزانُ
في كل مكانٍ روحٌ تصرخُ في الظُلُماتْ
في كلِّ مكانٍ يبكي صوتْ
هذا ما قد مزَّقَهُ الموتْ
الموتُ الموتُ الموتْ
يا حُزنَ النيلِ الصارخِ ما فعلَ الموتْ

طَلَعَ الفجرُ
أصغِ إلى وَقعِ خُطَى الماشينْ
في صمتِ الفجرِ ، أصِخْ ، أنظرْ ركبَ الباكين
عشرةُ أمواتٍ ، عشرونا
لا تُحصِ أصِخْ للباكينا
إسمعْ صوتَ الطفلِ المسكين
مَوتَى ، مَوتَى ، ضاعَ العددُ
مَوتَى ، موتَى ، لم يَبْقَ غَدُ
في كلِّ مكانٍ جَسَدٌ يندُبهُ محزونْ
لا لحظةَ إخلادٍ لا صَمْتْ
هذا ما فعلتْ كفُّ الموتْ

they are dead, they are dead, they are dead,
all humanity protests the crimes death commits

cholera
in the terrible caves where the corpses are piled
in eternity's hush, where death acts as a cure
cholera lies awake
unavenged, overflowing with hate
pouring over the valley's sweet, radiant soil
crying out, agitated, insane
it is deaf to the voices that mourn
as its talons leave scars everywhere
in the poor peasant's shack, in the landowner's house
nothing but cries of death, pouring out,
they are dead, they are dead, they are dead
as death takes its revenge wearing cholera's face

silence, still
nothing left but the trace of *Allahu akbar*
as the gravedigger too lies in eternal sleep
there is no one to help
the muezzin is dead
who will eulogize them?
nothing left now but shuddering sobs
the poor child has no mother, no dad
and tomorrow disease will no doubt snatch him too

الموتُ الموتُ الموتُ
تشكو البشريّةُ تشكو ما يرتكبُ الموتُ

الكوليرا
في كَهْفِ الرعبِ مع الأشلاءِ
في صَمْتِ الأبدِ القاسي حيثُ الموتُ دواءُ
استيقظَ داءُ الكوليرا
حقداً يتدفّقُ موتورا
هبطَ الوادي المرحَ الوَضّاءِ
يصرخُ مضطرباً مجنونا
لا يسمعُ صوتَ الباكينا
في كلِّ مكانٍ خلّفَ مخلبُهُ أصداء
في كوخ الفلّاحةِ في البيتِ
لا شيءَ سوى صرَخات الموتْ
الموتُ الموتُ الموتُ
في شخص الكوليرا القاسي ينتقمُ الموتْ

الصمتُ مريرْ
لا شيءَ سوى رجْعِ التكبيرْ
حتّى حَفّارُ القبرِ ثوَى لم يبقَ نَصيرْ
الجامعُ ماتَ مؤذّنُهُ
الميّتُ من سيؤبّنُهُ
لم يبقَ سوى نَوْحٍ وزفيرْ
الطفلُ بلا أمٍّ وأبِ
يبكي من قلبٍ ملتهبِ
وغداً لا شكَّ سيلقفُهُ الداءُ الشرّيرْ

evil cholera, what have you done?
you've left nothing in Egypt but sadness and death
they are dead, they are dead, they are dead
this is what death has done, and my heart is in shreds

1947

يا شبَحَ الهيْضنة ما أبقيتَ
لا شيءَ سوى أحزانِ الموتْ
الموتُ ، الموتُ ، الموتْ
يا مصرُ شعوري مزَّقَهُ ما فعلَ الموتْ

١٩٤٧

A Funeral for Happiness

I'll close my window on the lights that taint this chilly dark
and draw the curtains on the pages of an ancient tale
drive out the dull voice of the wind and the rays of the
    rancorous stars
to rest my head on memories, immerse my eyes in tears
to wrap the victim in my love and warm his lifeless face
if only I could bring him back, wipe the blue from his lips.

I'll close my window – he prefers the deepest, deepest dark
I'd hate for light to stretch its limbs across his poet's corpse
face tilled and sown by stars and lustrous with their dappled
    light
once radiating life, now wracked with suffering and pain
where death's hand writes the lines of stories from a distant age
I pass my hand over the skin and scream, collapse in dust.

I'll close my window tight against the malice of midday
pouring out cold tranquility, mocking me with its rage
its endless silence hunts me down, color of sediment
depressing me – where should I run? This room's dark stabs
    the drapes –
where should I run? I'm frightened by the paleness his face
dead man before me, daylight at my back – unhappy chase.

جنازة المرح

يعكّـر ظلمــتي البـارده	ســأغلق نافــذتي فالضيــاء
على صفحةِ القصةِ البائده	سأسـدل هذا الستار السميك
وإشــعاعةَ الأنجـمِ الحاقـده	وأطـردُ صوتَ الـرياح البليد
وأغمـس عينيّ في دمعتينْ	وأُسنـدُ رأسي إلى الذكريات
ويُـذفئُ جبهتهُ الهامـده	وأرسـلُ حبي يلـفُّ القتيل
وأمسـحُ مـن زُرقةِ الشفتينْ	لعـلّي أردُّ إليـه الحيــاة

يحبُ الظلام العميق العميق	ســأغلقُ نافــذتي فالقتيــل
على جسمه الشاعريّ الرقيق	وأكـرَهُ أن يتمـطى الضياء
ولوّنهـا ضوؤها بالبريـقْ	على جبهةٍ زرعتها النجـوم
تمجُ الأسى والرّدى والعـذابْ	وكانـت تُشِعُّ الحيـاةَ فعـادت
أساطيرَ عهـدٍ سحيقٍ سحيقْ	تخـطُّ عليهـا ذراعُ الممـات
خُ رعباً وأسقط فوق الترابْ	أمـرُّ عليهـا بكـفِّي فـأصرُ

ةُ لا ينتهي حقدُها الراعب	ســأغلقُ نافــذتي فالظهـير
ويسخرُ بي وجهُها الغاضبُ	تصبُ سكينتها في بـرودٍ
ويكئبـني لونها الراسـبُ	يطاردُني صمتها السرمديُّ
تدخلها غرفتي المظلمـه	وأينَ المفـرُّ؟ تكاد الستائرُ
يروِعـني وجهـه الشاحبُ	وأين المفـرُّ؟ وهـذا القتيـلُ
ةُ يا للمطـاردةِ المؤلمــه	أمـامي القتيل وخلـفي الظهير

61

I'll wait for light to fall behind the world and darkness come
to drag the victim out of evening's caves, to the abyss
and walk in the procession, footsteps slow as winter nights
while gasps of anxious, aimless memory proceed with me
indifferent escorts to the corpse in the reeling cortege
unfeeling escorts to the corpse in the reeling cortege.

I knew his brow, his lips, I knew those viscous, filmy eyes
in them I saw the sadness I had buried coming back
the same old wound, knife of my pain-filled past still caked
    with blood
I saw my fearless foe there, in the wake of the parade
mocking the victim, laughing in his sinful way, oh yes,
it's him, I know him well, he's crossed my path a thousand
    times.

Behind, I saw a thousand ghosts shrouded in mournful tears
In them I recognized the smiles with which I met life's blows
and recognized the laughs whose dew watered my memories
Is this what my smiles want? To turn love into echoed sighs?
Is this what laughter wanted? The cruel fate of every smile?
Have I interred my fleeting happiness beside this corpse?

1948

سـأصبرُ حـتى يجيءَ الـدُّبَى | ويغرب خلف الوجود الضياءُ
فأحـمـلُ هـذا القتيلَ البريءَ | إلى هـوَّةٍ مـن كهـوف المساءُ
أسيـرُ بأشـلائه موكبـاً | بطيءَ الخطى كليالي الشتاءُ
وتتبعـني شَـهقاتُ التذكّـ | ـرِ مهمومةً في أسئٍ وشرود
وفي آخِـر الموكب المترنّح | وجـهٌ يشيّعُـهُ في ازدراءُ
وفي آخِـرِ الموكـب المـترنّحِ | وجـهٌ يشّعُـهُ في بُـرُودْ

عرفـتُ الجبينَ عرت الشفاه | وهـذي العيون الغـلاظ الأديمْ
عرفـتُ بها وجه حزني الدفين | وقـد عادَ يحملُ جرحيَ القديم
وفي يَـده مُدية لم يَـزَلْ | على حدّها دمُ أمسيَ الأليمْ
عرفـتُ العدوَّ اللجوجَ هناك | يسـيرُ عـلى أثـر الموكـب
يُحـدِّقُ مستهزئاً بالقتيـل | ويضحك ضحكـة فظٍّ أثيمْ
نعـم هـوَ ... أعرفه جيداً | فكَم مـرةٍ قـبـلُ قـد مرَّ بي

وأبصرتُ في أثري ألف طيفٍ | حـزينٍ تلفّـعَ بالعـبراثْ
عرفتُ بها البساتِ التـي | لَقيتُ بها لَطَماتِ الحياة
عرفـتُ بها الضّحِكات التـي | سكبتُ نداها على الذكريات
أهـذي إذنُ بساتي؟ حنـاناً | أعـدْن عبوساً ورجُعَ أنين؟
أهـذي إذن ضحكاتي أهـذي | نهايةُ ما صُغتُ مـن بسمات
وهذا القتيـلُ أحقّـاً فقـدْتُ | بـه مـرَحي المضمحلَّ الدفين؟

١٩٤٨

Accusations

I express everything that I feel in my life
paint my strange spirit's feelings in color
and I cry when the many long years lunge at me
with their frightening, eternal daggers
and I laugh at the fate that cruel time has decreed
for the wondrous human frame
and get angry when feelings are trampled or mocked,
as though they were not rivers of flame.
I express everything that I sense
and I cry when life's blows make me reel
and I laugh at the strangest things in it
and get angry sometimes,
but I feel.

"She's a poet who's stuck in the clouds," they all say,
"in mirages of stars, there she floats.
She is selfish and disconnected from the world
as it wrestles with mountains of woe.
Prone to fantasy, she builds her world out of mist,
and despises the world of the living.
Melancholy, she hates anybody who laughs
as she buries her pale face in grieving."
Yes, I'm selfish, I love humankind
prone to dreams, yes, but my life goes on,
Melancholy, yes, I speak with flowers
My emotions are feelings aflame.

تهم

أعـبّر عمّـا تُحـسّ حَيـاتي   وأرسمُ إحساسَ روحي الغريبْ

فأبـكي إذا صدمتـني السنين   بخَنْجرهـا الأبـديّ الرهيـبْ

وأضحَـكُ ما قضاهُ الزمـان   على الهيكل الآدميّ العجيبْ

وأغضَبُ حين يُدَاسُ الشعور   ويُسخَرُ من فَوَرانِ اللهيبْ

أعـبّرُ عـن كلِّ حـسٍّ أعيـهْ

وأبـكي الحيـاةَ ولا أنكِـرُ

وأضحَـك مـن كلِّ مـا تحتويهْ

وأغضَـبُ لكنّـني أشعُـرُ

يقولـون شاعرةٌ في السَحاب   تحلّـقُ خلفَ سَراب النجومْ

أنانيّـةٌ لا تُحـسُّ الوجـود   وإن صرعتهُ جبـالُ الغمومْ

خياليّـةٌ تمقُتُ الكائنـات   وتخلُـقُ عالَمها في الغُيومْ

خريفيّـةٌ تكرَهُ الضاحكين   لتدفِـنَ جبهتَهـا في الهُمومْ

أنانيّـةٌ وأحِـبُّ البَـشَرْ

خياليّـةٌ وحيـاتي تَسيـرْ

خريفيّـةٌ وأنـاجي الزَهَـرْ

وعاطفتي لَهَبٌ من شُعُوزْ

65

They say, "She is a woman in love with the dark,
adores shadows, is smitten with still,
spends her life singing poems to fresh mountain streams
and describing her dreams to the hills.
She loves life, but she muddies its waters
by forever imagining death."
I love darkness, yes, I will admit it
it is only your dreams that I hate.
I love life and everything in it
but I recoil from your days' parade.

"All her feelings are frozen," they say, "and she lives
with the past in a frozen dream."
"She's a Sufi," they say, "and her senses are dead
as she loses them her life will scream.
Her emotions are frigid, icier than stars
or the cold lullaby of the moon.
Though she had a brief flight, still her unmoving heart
brought her down from the sky all too soon."
So they say, as I wander through silence
sheltered, warmed by the hidden and strange
living life like the gods, with my heart full of feeling
and my spirit aflame.

يقولونَ: عاشقةٌ للظلامِ تُحبُّ الـدياجي وتَهْوَى السُكونْ
وتُنْشِـدُ أشـعارَها للجبالِ   وتَرْسُـمُ أحلامَهـا للعيـونْ
تحـبُّ الحيـاةَ ولكنَّهـا   تُعكِّرُها بخيالِ المَنونْ
تـرَى جوَّها غيهبـاً حالكاً   يضيـقُ بآثامِهِ المُلهَمونْ

أحـبُّ الظـلامَ ولكنـني
أثـورُ عـلـى كلِّ أحلامِكـمْ
أحبُّ الحيـاةَ عـلى أنني
أحقِّـرُ موكـبَ أيامِكـمْ

يقولونَ: جامـدةُ الحسِّ تَحْيا   مـع الأمسِ في حُلُمٍ جامدِ
يقولونَ: صوفيَّـةٌ فالحيـاةُ   تنـوحُ عـلى جِثِّها الخامدِ
عواطفُهـا جَمَـدَتْ كالنجومِ   كتهويمـةِ القَمَـرِ الباردِ
وتحـليقُهـا كانَ ثـم انْمَحى   على صَدرِ إحساسِها الراكدِ

يقولـونَ لكنَّـني تائهـهْ
ألوذُ بصَمتِ الخفيِّ الغريبْ
أعيـشُ حيـاتي كالآلهـهْ
وقلـبي شعورٌ وروحي لهيبْ

So they say – leave them be, they will soon understand
and leave me to beauty and perfume
I love life in the depths of my heart, and I blend
its reality with these dreams.
My deep passion for nature has nearly made me mad
I love date-palms, and mountains, and willows,
and I love myself, because I know in my depths
there's a fantasy world steeped in shadows.
I cry out to the fire in this heart
and the wave of feelings in revolt
they accuse me, I only reply
with this mocking and sarcastic smile.

1947

يقولـون دَعهـم غـداً يعلمـون   ودعـني أنا للشَّـذى والجمـالُ
أحبُّ الحيـاةَ بقلبي العميـق   وأمــزُجُ واقعَهـا بالخيـالُ
أحبُّ الطبيعـةَ حُبَّ جنون   أحبُّ النخيلَ أحبُّ الجبالُ
وأعشَــقُ ذاتي فـي عُمقهـا   خيـالُ وجـودٍ عميقِ الظلالُ
وأهتِـفُ يا نارَ قلبي الغريـب
ومــوجَ أحاسـيسي الثائِره
إذا اتَّهمـوا فلمـاذا أُجيـبْ
بغـيرِ ابتسـامتي السـاخِرَه؟

١٩٤٧

POEMS FROM
AT THE BOTTOM OF THE WAVE
(1957)

قصائد من
قـرارة الموجـة
(۱۹۵۷)

To a Girl Sleeping in the Street

In Karrada at night, wind and rain before dawn,
when the dark is a roof or a drape never drawn,

when the night's at its peak and the dark's full of rain,
and the wet silence roils like a fierce hurricane,

the lament of the wind fills the deserted street,
the arcades groan in pain, and the lamps softly weep.

A guard frowns as he passes with trembling steps,
lightning shows his thin frame, but shadows intercept.

Swept away by the floods, torn to bits by the cold,
the night trembles with dark, shivers when thunder rolls.

At a bend in the road, the threshold of a door
to a house that nobody lives in anymore,

lightning flashes and shows, lying there, fast asleep
a young girl, skin ripped raw by the winter wind's whip.

In her eyes' innocence, in the pale of her cheeks,
the thinness of her frame, her eleven years speak.

النائمة في الشارع

في الكَـرّادةِ، في ليـلةِ أمطـارٍ ورياحٍ
والظلمةُ سقفٌ مُدّ وسترٌ ليس يُـزَاحُ

انتصَفَ الليلُ وملءُ الظلمةِ أمطارُ
وسكونٌ رطـبٌ يـصرخُ فيه الإعصارُ

الشـارعُ مهجـورٌ تُعـولُ فيـه الـريحُ
تتوجَّـع أعـمـدةٌ وتنـوحُ مصابيـحُ

والحارس يَعبرُ جَهْماً مرتعدَ الخُطُواتْ
يكشِفُهُ البرقُ وتحجُبُ هيكلَه الظُلُماتْ

ليـلٌ يجرفُـهُ السيلُ وينهَشُـهُ البَرْدُ
تنتفِـضُ الظلمـةُ فيـه ويرتعـشُ الرعدُ

في مُنعَطَفِ الشارعِ، في ركنٍ مقرورٍ
حَرَسَتْ ظُلمَتَه شرفةُ بيتٍ مهجورِ

كان البرقُ يمرُّ ويكشفُ جسمَ صبيه
رقدتْ يلسَعُها سوطُ الريحِ الشتويه

الإحـدَى عـشـرةَ ناطقـةٌ في خَدّيهـا
في رقَّـةِ هيكلهـا وبـراءةِ عينيهـا

She sleeps there, on the frozen asphalt of the ground,
while around her small form the November wind howls,

tiny hands clasped so tight in exhaustion and fear,
the wet pavement her pillow, her blanket the air.

She can't sleep from the fever, the thunder, the flame
that insomnia lights deep inside her small frame.

She is thirsty for sleep, but sleep never takes hold.
What should she forget first – fever, hunger, or cold?

Twice redoubled by sleeplessness, still the pain gnaws
reignited by fever with merciless claws.

With their devilish screams, these harsh pictures inspire
specters rushing around to feed the fever's fire,

and she covers her eyes, but her hands can't conceal
that the dark doesn't know, and the fever can't feel.

The small girl goes on trembling until the sun shows,
'til the hurricane dies down, and still no one knows.

رَقَدَتْ فوقَ رخامِ الأرصفةِ الثلجيَّه
تُعوِلِ حــولَ كَرَاهـا ريحٌ تشرينيَّـه

ضَمَّـتْ كفَّيْهـا في جَــزَعٍ في إعيــاءٍ
وتوسَّـدتِ الأرضَ الرطبـةَ دون غطـاءِ

لا تغفو ، لا تَغفُلُ عن إعوالِ الرَّعدِ
والحـمّى تُلهبُ هيكلها ويـدُ السَّهدِ

ظمـأى ، ظمـأى للنـومِ ولكـن لا نومـا
ماذا تنسى؟ البردُ؟ الجوعُ؟ أمِ الحمّى؟

ألمٌ يبـقَى ينهـشُ ، لا يرحَـمُ مِخْلَبُـهُ
السَّهـدُ يضاعفـهُ والحــمّى تُلهبُـهُ

نـارُ الحمّى تُلهمُها صوراً وحشيَّه
أشباحٌ بركُضُ ، صيحاتٌ شيطانيَّه

عبثاً تُخْفي عينَيها وسُدىً لا تَنْظُـرُ
الظلمـة لا تـدري ، والحـمّى لا تشعُرُ

وتَظَـل الطفلةُ راعشـةً حتى الفجـرِ
حتى يخبو الإعصارُ ولا أحدٌ يدري

She spent every day of her childhood in tears
body broken by homelessness, hunger, and fear,

for eleven long years, sadness never expired
her whole life she was hungry, and thirsty, and tired.

To whom should she protest? Her cries all go unheard,
for *humanity*'s now just a meaningless word,

and *people* are a mask, artificial and fake,
their sweet, gentle exteriors hide burning hate,

and where *mercy* once thrived in our society
now it's merely a word in the dictionary.

Those who sleep on the street will remain discontent,
no one pities their fevers or soothes their laments –

it is savage injustice, no consideration –
what a farce that we call this world *civilization*!

أيّــامُ طفولتهــا مــرّت في الأحــزانِ
تشريـدٌ، جوعٌ، أعوامٌ من حِرمـانِ

إحدَى عشرةَ كانتْ حزْناً لا ينطفئُ
والطفلـةُ جـوعٌ أزليٌّ، تَعَـبٌ، ظَمَـأٌ

ولمن تشكو؟ لا أحدٌ يُنصِتُ أو يُغْني
البشريّــةُ لفــظٌ لا يسـكُنُه معنـى

والناس قنـاعٌ مصطنعُ اللونِ كَذُوبُ
خلفَ وداعتِهِ اختبأ الحِقْد المشبوبُ

والمجتمع البَشَريُّ صريعُ رؤىً وكؤوسٍ
والرحمة تبـقى لفظاً يُقْرأ في القاموسِ

ونيـامٌ في الشـارع يبقَـوْنَ بـلا مـأوى
لا حُـمَى تشفَعُ عند الناسِ ولا شكوى

هـذا الظُلْمُ المتوحـشُ باسـم المدنيّـه،
باسم الإحساسِ، فوا تَحَجّلَ الإنسانيّه

Elegy for a Woman of No Importance

(OR, IMAGES FROM A BAGHDAD ALLEYWAY)

She died, but no lips shook, no cheeks turned white
no doors heard her death tale told and retold,
no blinds were raised for sad eyes to behold
the casket as it disappeared from sight.
Only a beggar in the street, consumed
by hunger, heard the echo of her life –
the safe forgetfulness of tombs,
the melancholy of the moon.

The night gave way to morning thoughtlessly,
and light brought with it sound – boys throwing stones,
a hungry, mewling cat, all skin and bones,
the vendors fighting, clashing bitterly,
some people fasting, others wanting more,
polluted water gurgling, and a breeze
playing, alone, upon the door
having almost forgotten her.

July 9 1952

مرثية امرأة لا قيمة لها

"صور من زقاق بغداديّ"

ذهبت ولم يَشحَبْ لهـا خدٌّ ولم ترجفْ شفاهُ
لم تَسمع الأبـوابُ قصةَ موتهـا تُروَى وتُروَى
لم ترتفعْ أستار نافـذةٍ تسيلُ أسئً وشَجُـوا
لتتابـعَ التابـوت بالتحديـقِ حتى لا تـراه
إلا بقيّـةَ هيـكلٍ في الـدربِ تُرعِشُـه الذِّكَرْ
نبـأ تعثّـرَ في الـدروب فـلم يجدْ مـأوىً صداهُ
فأوَى إلى النسيانِ في بعضِ الحُفَرْ
يـــرثي كأبَّتَـــه القَمَـــرْ

والليـلُ أسـلمَ نفسَـهُ دون اهتمامٍ ، للصَبـاحْ
وأتى الضياءُ بصوتِ بائعةِ الحليبِ وبالصيامْ ،
بمُـوَاءِ قـطٍّ جائـعٍ لم تَبْـقَ منـه سـوى عظامْ ،
بمُشـاجراتِ البائِعَـين ، وبالمـرارة والكفـاحْ
بتراشُـقِ الصبيان بالأحجار في عُـرضِ الطريقْ ،
بمسـاربِ المـاء الملـوِّثِ في الأزقّـةِ ، بالريـاحْ
تلهـو بأبـوابِ السطوح بـلا رفيـقْ
في شـــبهِ نسـيانٍ عميـــقْ.

٩ تموز ١٩٥٢

THREE ELEGIES FOR MY MOTHER

For those who are happy, poetry may be merely a mental luxury, but for those who are sad, it becomes a way of life. The following three poems were my attempt to mourn my mother, who died in sad circumstances that caused me great suffering. There was no other outlet for my pain; I had to love it and sing to it.

N.M.

ثلاثُ مَرَاثٍ لأُمِّي

قد يكون الشـعر بالنسبة للإنسـان السـعيد ترفاً ذهنياً محضاً ، غير أنه بالنسبة للمحـزون وسـيلة حيـاة. وقـد كانت القصائـد الثلاث التالية محـاولة للتعزي لجـأتُ إليهـا عـلى إثر وفـاة أمي في ظروف محزنـة عانيت منها معـاناة خاصة. ولم أجد لألمي منـفذاً آخر غـير أن أحبـه وأغني له.

ن. م.

I. A Song for Sadness

Make way for one whose feelings show,
young swimmer in a fragrant sea,
who traversed time's fertility
and stole the secrets of the snow
    as quiet as a stream
    don't wound him with your screams.

A boy who's melancholy, shy,
who dwells in evenings drenched in sadness,
corners dark with twilight stillness,
never cowed by mournful cries.
    Our silence gives him shade
    and a hidden embrace.

He lives inside our speechless tears,
has hidden homes in distant depths,
known only to those who have wept
in silence, not for listening ears.
    He feeds on quiet pains
    concealed within our veins.

١. أغنية للحزن

أفسحوا الدرْبَ له ، للقادم الصافي الشعورِ ،
للغلام المُرهَفِ السابحِ في بحـرِ أريــجٍ ،
ذي الجبـين الأبيـض السارق أسرارَ الثلوجِ
إنّـه جـاء إلينـا عابراً خضْبَ المُـرورِ
إنّـه أهـدأ مـن مـاءِ الغـديرِ
فاحـذَروا أن تجرحوه بالضجيجِ

إنّـه ذاكَ الغـلامُ الدائمُ الحُـزْنِ الخجـولُ
سـاكنُ الأُمسيـةِ الغَـرْقى بأحـزانٍ خفيّـه
والـزوايا الغيـبيّـاتِ السكونِ الشَفَقيّه
أبـداً يجرحـه النَـوْحُ ويُضنيـهِ العويـلُ
فليكـن من صمتنا ظـلٌّ ظليـلُ
يتلقّـاه وأحضـانٌ خفيّـه

وهو يحيا في الدموع الخُرْس في بعضِ العيونِ
ولهُ كـوخٌ خـفيٍّ شِـيـدَ في عُمـقٍ سحيـقٍ
ضائـعٌ يعرفُـه الباكـون في صمْتٍ عميـقٍ
وسُـدىً يبحثُ عنـه الألمُ الخشـنُ الرنينِ
إنّـه يقتـات أسـرارَ السكونِ
وأسى مختبئـاً خلـفَ العـروقِ

For him we have prepared an ode
our ready lips and eyes will greet him
as one meets a god, we'll meet him
though our perfumed tears explode.
    We'll give him grieving brows
    stronger and stronger now.

More beautiful than love, than art,
he is a lily death has thrown
into our hands, and we alone
give it a place in every heart.
    He is of us, we've learned,
    and to us he's returned.

August 15 1953

نحـــن هيّــأنا له حبّــاً وتقديساً ونجـــوى

وتهيّـــأنا للُقيـــاه عيـــوناً وشـــفاها

وسنُلْقاه مُصَلّـــينَ كما نلـــقَى إلهـــا

وسنُهديه انفجـــارَ الأدمـع العَذبـة سلوى

وسنحبوه أسىً أقـــوى وأقـــوى

وسنُغطيه عُيـــوناً وجباهـــا

إنّه أجمـــل مـــن أفراحنـــا، مـــن كلّ حُـبّ

إنّـــه زنبقـــةٌ ألـــقى بهـــا المـــوت علَينـــا

لم تـــزَل دافئـــةً ترعـــش في شوق يدَيْنـــا

وسنُعطيها مـــكاناً عطِـــراً في كلّ قلـــب

وشذَى حُزْنٍ عميق القَعْرِ خِضْـــبِ

إنّـــه منـــا ... وقد عـــاد إلينـــا

١٥ آب ١٩٥٣

II.   The Arrival of Sadness

Make way, he's here – soft-footed, shy, and sad
the sensitive young man, his eyes submerged
in stories of a thousand tragic secrets
he feeds deep eyes, he is the spring of tears
he's come to us across the years
mute droplets in his eyes.

Our youthful sadness – we've met him before
without appointment or anticipation
he is still quiet, shy, just as he was,
still hiding secrets and still warm – he's come
softer than tears, sweeter than strings
humming with tunes, we laid a path
for him made out of sighs, and love, and tears.

We humbly carried him down to the depths
of our dream-visions and our happiness
and gave him all the colors and perfume
that love once gathered up out of our youth.
Stone next to stone, we laid the hopes that death
and pain had left to us to form a path
and washed his brow in silent, thirsty tears.

He is our last thread to the cypress tree.
In him a thousand memories from the past
lie dormant. Still he whispers, "she is dead"
till light and scent and everyone have heard.
In him warm remnants of her face remain,
her hopes, her longing too – he is the whole
feeling of her, come back to make every
last fiber of our being quake.

٢. مقدم الحزن

نَ رقيقَ الخُطى كئيب الجبينِ	أفسحوا الدربَ ، إنّه جاء نجلا
قى بتاريخ ألفِ سرٍّ حزينِ	الغلامُ الحسّاس ذو الأعين الغر
تِ وينبوعُ كلِّ دمعٍ سخينِ	إنه مُطعمُ العيونِ العميقا
هِ الدموعُ الخرساءُ عبر السنينِ	ولقـد جـاءنا تُبلّـلُ عينيـ

ه على غير موعدٍ وانتظارِ	إنّه حزنُنا الصبيّ لَقينا
نَ وما زال غامـقَ الأسرارِ	لم يَزَل هادئاً نجهـولاً كا كا
ـعَ وأحلى مـن رعُشـةِ الأوتارِ	جاءنا دافئاً أرقَّ مـن الدَمـ
ـفةٍ والحبّ والدمـوع الغزارِ	ففرشـنا له طريقـاً مـن اللَهـ

ـماقِ أفراحنا وقَعـرُ رؤانا	وأخـذناه في خشوعٍ إلى أعـ
من اللـونِ والشَـذَى لصبانا	ومنحنـاه كلّ مـا جمـع الحب
ـقى لنا الموتُ والأسى مـن مُنانا	ورصفنـا له هـوانا ومـا أبـ
صامتاتٍ عطْشى تـذوبُ حنانا	وغسـلنا جبينَـه بدمـوع

وةٍ فيه من أمسنا ألفُ شيءٍ	إنّه خيطنـا الأخيرُ إلى السَرْ
تثُ على مسمع الشذَى والضوءِ	لم يَزَل هامسـاً لنـا: "إنها ما
ـها وأشواقِها بقيّـةَ دفْءٍ	إنّ فيه مـن وجهِها وأمانيـ
مُرعِشاً مـن كياننا كلَّ جزءٍ	وهـو إحسـاسُها يعـود إلينا

87

He is all that remains of laughter's face
and echoed songs. He is the end result
of all the hopes that cruel death destroyed.
We offered him shy prayers made of tears
and whispered melodies, we offered him
a home inside the corners of our eyes
and a love stronger than forgetfulness.

August 17 1953

إنـه كـلُّ مـا تبـقَّى لنـا مـن   وجـه ضِحْكاتنـا ورجْـع الأغـاني

إنَّ فيـه نهايـةَ الطَـرَف الثـا   نـي لِمـا هـدَّم الـرَدَى مـن أمـانِ

فوهبنـا لـه صـلاةً مـن الأد   مـع تَجَـلّى مهموسـةَ الألحـانِ

ومنحنـاه مسـكناً في مآقيـ   ـنا وحُبّاً أقوى مـن النسيانِ

١٧ آب ١٩٥٣

III.   The Black Flower

We left our dearest treasure here,
then hurried back after a time
and searched for it both far and near,
but found nothing behind the rise.

We stopped to ask a forest hill
and whispered in the cypress' ear:
the first said that she'd never tell,
the last pretended not to hear.

But dawn sustained us with her light
and showed us in the treasure's place
a flower: black, as dark as night,
watered with tears, showing her face.

When visited by morning winds,
she fills the air with melody,
and hides inside her quiet hymns
the tears of all humanity.

She is our sad and sleepy flower:
her black petals hold our past.
We cried for her, then carried her
with memory, then left at last.

August 31 1953

٣. الزهرة السوداء

كــنزنا الغـــالي تركنـــاه هُنـا
لحظــاتٍ ثم أسرعنـــا إليــه
والتمســـناه وراء المُنْحَـــنى
وعـلى التـلّ فـلم نعـثر عليـهِ

وسـألْنا عنـه في الغابـة ربـوه
فأجابــتْ أنـهـا قـد نَسِـيَتْه
وهمسْـنا باسمـه في سَمع سَرْوه
فتناسـتْ في الدُّجى ما سمعتْه

غير أنَّ الفجر حتى في ابتسـام
وأرانا في مـكان الكـنزِ زهـره
نبتت سوداءَ في لون الظلامْ
وسـقاها دمعُنـا لينـاً ونَطْره

كُلّمـا مـرّت بهـا ريح الصبـاحْ
بعثـتْ في الجوّ موسيقى خفيّةْ
وأنينـاً خافتـا ملءَ الـريـاخ
كمنـتْ فيـه دمـوع البشريّـه

إنهـا زهرتُنـا الوسـنى الحزينه
أمسُـنا في لونِها مـا زال لَذْنا
فمنحناها مآقينـا السخينه
وحملناها مع الذكرى وعُدْنا

٣١ آب ١٩٥٣

91

Killing a Dancer

To the girl with the sacrificed heart, dance and sing
and rejoice, for the wound is a dance and a smile
ask the victimized dead to sleep on for a while
as you dance, beautiful, reassured, dance and sing.

Are those tears in your eyes? Wipe away their hot pain
and squeeze out a sweet smile from the scream of your wound.
An explosion? The wound is asleep, makes no sound,
leave it here and surrender to your hateful chains.

Revolution? Come now, let the whip lash at you –
of what use are a victim's convulsions and cries?
For the world will forget, in the fullness of time,
some sad things, some disasters, a dead man or two.

Turn the burn of your wounds into a lovely air,
let it pour from your parched mouth and suffuse the room.
There is still enough life on your lips for a tune
that does not overflow with sadness and despair.

Are those screams? What ingratitude! You must be mad!
Leave your dead lying here, unburied, on the ground.
Of what use is a prisoners' uprising now?
Only one person died, there's no need to be sad.

الراقصة المذبوحة

أرقصي مذبوحـة القلـب وغـنّي
واضحـكي فالجُرح رَقْصٌ وابتسـامُ
اسألي الموتَى الضحايا أن ينامـوا
وارقـصي أنـتِ وغـنّي واطمئـنّي

أدموعٌ؟ أسكتي الدمعَ السخينا
واعصُري من صرخة الجُرح ابتساما
أانفجـارٌ؟ هـدأ الجُـرح ونامـا
فاتركيـه واعبُـدي القيـدَ المُهينـا

ثورةٌ؟ لا تُبغضي السوطَ المُلحّا
أيّ معنىً لاختلاجـاتِ الضحايا؟
بعـض أحـزانٍ سـتُنسى ، ورزايـا
وقتيـلٌ أو قتيـلان ، وجَـرحى

إقبِسي من جُرحِكِ المُحرق لحنا
رتّميـه بالشِّـفـاهِ الظامئـاتِ
لم تـزلْ فيهـا بقايـا مـن حيـاةِ
لنشيـدٍ لم يَفِـضْ بؤساً وحُـزنا

صرخـةٌ؟ أيّ جمـودٍ وجُنـونٍ !
أتـركي قَتْـلاكِ صَرعَى دون دفـنٍ
واحـدٌ مات ... فـلا صرخةَ حزنٍ !
أيّ معنىً لانتفاضـات السجين ؟

An uprising, you say? Is there any blood left
flowing through the dry remnants of your people's veins?
And explosions? Do any innocents remain
to be turned into victims who've not been killed yet?

No, your wound was not rare among all other wounds,
so drink deeply of this lethal sadness and dance
as the slaves stand confused to the point of silence –
are you protesting? Why? Just relax and resume

and laugh out loud with love at the dagger stained red,
then collapse on the ground as though you're fast asleep.
It is good for you to be slaughtered like a sheep,
good for spirit and heart to be penetrated,

it is madness for victims like you to rebel
and the prisoners' hatred is madness as well.
Go on, dance now, be happy and kind in your way,
and smile on with the joy of a laboring slave.

Time to silence your wound, there's no moaning allowed,
time to smile at your killer, be charming and sweet,
time to give him your heart, disgraced, broken, and free,
get him drunk stabbing, ripping, and tearing you down,

انتفاضاتٌ؟ وفي الشَّعبِ بقايا
مـن عـروقٍ لم تَسلْ نبعَ دمـاءٍ؟
انفجـاراتٌ؟ وبعـض الأبـريـاءِ
بعضُهـم لم يسقُطوا بعْدُ ضحـايا؟

لم يكـن جُرحُكِ بذعـاً في الجُروحِ
فارقُصي في سكرةِ الحزْنِ المميتِ
الأرقَّـاءِ الحيـارَى للسـكوتِ
احتجاجاتٌ؟ لـمـاذا؟ استريحي!

اضحـكي للمُذيـةِ الحمـراءِ حُبـا
واسـقُطي فوقَ الثرى دون اختلاجٍ
منّـةٌ أن تُـذبحي ذبحَ النعـاجِ
منّـةٌ أن تُطعـني روحـاً وقلبـاً

وجنـونٌ يا ضحـايا أن تثـوري
وجنـونٌ غضبـة الأسرى العبيـدِ
أُرقـصي رَقصة مُـمتنٍّ سـعيدِ
وابسـمي في غِبْطـة العبـد الأَجيـرِ

أسكتي الجُـرْحَ حَـرامٌ أن يئِنّـا
وابسمي للقاتـل الجـاني افتتـانا
امنحيـه قلبَـكِ الحـرّ المُلهـانا
ودعيـه ينتـشي حَـزّاً وَطغنـا

time to dance with your sacrificed heart, dance and sing
and rejoice, since the wound is a dance and a smile
ask the victimized dead to sleep on for a while
as you dance, beautiful, reassured, dance and sing.

1948

وارقصي مذبوحةَ القلب وغنّي
واضحكي فالجُرْحُ رَقصٌ وابتسامُ
اسألي الموتى الضحايا أن يناموا
وارقصي أنتِ وغنّي واطمئني

١٩٤٨

When I Killed My Love

How I hated you – nothing to save but this hate
which I water with blood to drown my present state
which I nourish with vengeance and curses and flames
and with screams of contempt heard in sad songs' refrains
I will feed it the sleep of the dead,
scatter ghosts and shadows on its bed.

How I hated your name, wished its echo such harm
hated color and song, hated rhythm and form
watched in joy as detestable, crude memories
fell corroded in graves next to eternities
I became a poem overheard
saying "yesterday's only a word."

You fell hard, like a statue, into the abyss,
and I buried your body under the cypress.
In the end, I had won – I had found victory
the shovel in my hand cleaved the earth greedily
till it struck a cold-footed body in the dirt
and I happily dragged it out into the light
But whose body was it?
                           Just the corpse of regret.

عندما قتلت حبي

وأبغضتُك لم يبقَ سوى مَقتي أناجيهِ
وأسقيهِ دماءَ غدي وأُغرِق حاضري فيهِ
وأطعمُه لظى اللَّعناتِ والثورةِ والنقمة
وأُسمعُهُ صراخَ الحِقْد في أغنيةٍ جَهمه
ومن إغفاءة الموتى أغنِّيهِ
وأنثر حولَه الأشباح والظلمه

وأبغضتُ اسمَكَ الملعونَ والأصداءَ والظلا
كرهت اللونَ النغمةَ والإيقاعَ والشكلا
وتلكَ الذكرياتُ الخشْنة الممقوتة الفظّه
هَوَتْ وتأكَّلتْ وثوثُ مع الآبادِ في لحظه
وعدتُ قصيدةً فجريةً جَذْلى
وقلتُ الأمسُ ما عاد سوى لفظه

وتمّ النصر لي وهَوَيْتَ تمثالاً إلى الهُوّه
وجئتُ لأُدفِنَ الأشلاءَ تحتَ كآبة السروه
وراح الرفش في كفي يشُقّ الأرض في نَهَم
فلامسَ في الثرى جسداً رهيباً بارد القدَم
ورحت أجرّه للضوءِ مَزْهوّه
فمن كان؟
بقايا جُثّة النَدَم

99

Then the night was a mirror where I saw all my hate
and my dead past, and everything but my true state.
I had just rid my evening and my cup of you
sent the body off gradually to its tomb
when I realized what I had done could never help –
for the only person I had killed was myself.

May 12 1952

وكان الليل مرآةً فأبصرت بها كُرْهِي
وأمسي الميْتَ لكنِّي لم أعثر على كُنْهِي
وكنت قتلتُكَ الساعةَ في ليلي وفي كأسي
وكنت أشيع المقتولَ في بُطْءٍ إلى الرمْسِ
فأدركت ولونُ اليأس في وجهي
بأني قطّ لم أقتلْ سوى نفسي

١٢ أيار ١٩٥٢

Words

I complained to the wind about my lonely heart
and it blew with the perfume of warm harvest nights,
and showered me sleepless with violet and rose,
and breathed sweet aromas to pillow my cheek,
quenched my longing with singing from valleys to brooks
and said, "These perfumed, colored ravines are for you,
and for your heart alone I have come to this world,
there is no need to cry."
I believed what they said.
Then the long evening came
and I asked if the winds had been telling the truth.
With a mocking expression, the darkness replied,
"You believed them? They were only words … "

At the dawn of my life, I was sung human songs
and took part as they danced in the pale moonlit night
and like them, I sang songs of sweet anticipation
of something to come, future Utopia
and believed that a dew-colored, flower-like life
would blot out all these days overburdened with grief.
When they told us that we were eternal in song,
that we're centuries old,
I believed what they said.
Then my friend evening came
tired, dragging its chains,
and I asked if humanity's songs were all true.
 "My dear girl," it exclaimed, staring in disbelief,
"You believed them? They were only words."

كلمات

شكوتُ إلى الريح وَحدةَ قلبي وطولَ انفرادي
فجاءت معطّرةً بأريــج ليـالي الحصادِ
وألقتْ عبيرَ البنفسَج والوردِ فوق سُهادي
ومدّت شَذاها لحدّي الكليلِ مكانَ الوسادِ
وروّت حنيـني بنجوى غـديرٍ يُغنّي لِوادِ
وقالـتْ: لأجلِكِ كان العبيـرُ ولونُ الوهادِ
ومن أجلِ قلبكِ وحدَكِ جئت الوجودَ الجميلْ
ففيمَ العويل؟
وصدَّقتُها ثم جاء المسـاءُ الطويـلْ
فساءلتُ ليلي: أحقٌّ حديثُ الرياحْ؟
فـرد الـدُّبى ساخرَ القَسَماتْ
"أصدَّقتِها؟ إنهـا كلمـاتْ ..."

وأصغيتُ في فجرِ عمري إلى أغنياتِ البَشرْ
وشاركتُهم رَقصَهم في شُحوبِ ليـالي القَمَـرْ
وغنيـتُ مثلَهُـم بالسعـادةِ، بالمُنتَظَـرْ
بـشيء سيأتي، بيوتوبيـا في سـنينٍ أُخرْ
وآمنـتُ أن حيـاةً بلـونِ النـدَى والزَهَـرْ
ستمسَـحُ أيامنـا المُثقَلات بعبءِ الضجرْ
وقالـوا لنـا في أغاريـدهم إننا خالـدونْ
خُلود القُرونْ
وصدقتُهم ثم جـاء المسـاءُ الصديـقْ
يجـرُ سلاسلَه في جمـودٍ وضيـقْ
فساءلتُهُ: أهوَ حقٌّ هُتـافُ البَشَرْ؟
فحـدّق بي صائحـاً: "يا فتـاةْ!
أصدّقتِهـمْ؟ إنهـا كلمـاتْ"

How often young lovers have tightened bright hopes,
squeezing death's honey out into fantasy's cups,
swearing eternal love by the stars in the sky,
by the dew on day's cheeks, by the evening's soft hush,
always vowing on love to be forever true,
that their love will remain even after life's death.
"For one love, everlasting," they said, "never dies,
defies loss, eases pain."
I believed what they said.
Then the kind evening came,
all shot through with the darkness of cool autumn nights
and I asked if the lovers' visions had been true.
"You believed them?" it muttered in soft, mocking tones,
"They were words ... "

May 28 1952

وكم مـرةٍ جَـدَل العاشقون الأمـاني الوِضـاء
وكم عـصروا في كـؤوس التخيّـل شهـدَ الوفـاء
وراحـوا عـلى حُبّهـم يُشهـدون نجـومَ السـماء
ووقّعَ النّدَى فوق خدّ الصباح، وصمتِ المساء
وكم أقسـموا بالهـوى أنّهـم أبـداً أوفيـاء
وأنّ الوجـودَ يمـوتُ وحبّهُـم للبقـاء
وقالـوا: هـوىً واحـدٌ خالـدٌ يتحـدّى العَـدَمْ
ويَـرضى الألم
وصدّقتُهـم ثم جـاء المسـاء اللطيـف
هنالكَ ذات دجئٍ من أماسي الخريف
وسـاءلتُهُ أهيَ حـقٌّ رؤى العاشقيْن؟
فغمغـمَ مسـتهزئَ النـبراث
"أصدّقتِهـم؟ إنّها كلمـات ..."

٢٨ أيار ١٩٥٢

An Invitation to Life

Get mad, I like when you resist
in burning, beautiful revolt,
I hate when fire sleeps in you
so be a blaze, glowing with pain.

Get mad, your spirit's almost dead
don't let me lose my storm inside
your silence, I'll be human ash
you be creation's blazing flame
inside my poetry.

Get mad, you've been weak long enough, and I don't like the weak.
Fire is righteous – stagnation and compromise are not.
I'm irritated by the sight of dignity's calm face
so I yelled "Death to ashes! And long live desire's flame!"
Reject this shameful silence
I cannot stand the quiet.

I like when you pulsate and move
a child, a violent wind, cruel fate
thirsty for glory when no bloom,
no scent can slake your visions' thirst.

دعوة إلى الحياة

اغضـبْ، أحبّـكَ غاضباً متمرّداً
في ثـــورةٍ مشـــبوبةٍ وتمـــزّق
أبغضتُ نومَ النار فيكَ فكن لظىً
كـن عـرْقَ شـوقٍ صارخٍ متحـرّق

اغضبْ، تكاد تموت روحُك، لا تكن
صمتاً أضيّـعُ عنـدَهُ إعصـاري
حسبي رَمادُ الناس، كن أنت اللظى
كـن حُرقة الإبـداع في أشـعاري

اغضبْ، كفاك وداعة. أنا لا أحبّ الوادعين
النّار شـرعي لا الجمـود ولا مهادَنـة السـنين
إني ضَجِرتُ من الوَقارِ ووجهِهِ الجهمِ الرصينْ
وصرختُ لا كان الرّماد وعاش عاش لَظى الحنينْ
اغضبْ على الصمتِ المُهينْ
أنـا لا أحبّ السـاكنينْ

إني أحبّـك نابضـاً، متحـــركا،
كالطفـل، كالـريح العنيفـةِ كالقَـدَرْ
عطشانَ للمجد العظيم فلا شذىً
يُـروي رؤاك الظامِئـاتِ ولا زهَـرْ

Patience? A virtue for the dead,
moldering in their frigid tombs
living under the reign of worms
they've gone to sleep, I give us life
as heat, as sparkling eyes and cheeks.

I like you best not when you preach, but when you feel the fear
inside the song and sing despite your thirst, with bloody throat
and burning vein. I like you when you scream at distant storms,
your melted mouth thawed out, rejuvenated by the flame,
where is your passion's fire?
I cannot stand the still.

Give us a frown, I'm sick of smiles
hills must be cold and warm in turn,
no spring can last forever, genius
lives in troubled minds.
I like you as an unquenched thirst
as the world ends, your spirit still
storms on, mad laughter, burning tear
a sacred quiet and a sense
of washing everything away.

I like the thirst of the volcano longing to erupt in you
the deep night's fierce desire for a meeting with the day
the overflowing spring's wish to be held in jars of clay
I want you as a bottomless river bursting with flame
get mad and curse at death
I am sick of the dead.

الصبرُ؟ تلك فضيلة الأموات ، في
بــرد المقـابـر تحـتَ حكم الـدودِ
رقـدوا وأُعطينـا الحيـاةَ حرارةً
نشـوى وحُرْقـةَ أعـين وخـدودِ

أنا لا أحبّـك واعظاً بـل شـاعراً قلـق النشيذ
تشدو ولو عطشانَ دامي الحلْق محترق الوريذ
إني أحبّـك صرخـةَ الإعصار في الأفق المديذ
وفمـاً تصبّـاه اللهيـب فبـات يحتقر الجليذ
أيــــن التحـــرّق والحنيــنْ؟
أنــا لا أطيـــق الراكديـنْ

قطّبْ ، سئمتُكَ ضاحكاً ، إنّ الرُّبَى
بــردُ ودفء لا ربيــعٌ خالــدُ
العبقريــة ، يا فتــايَ ، كئيبــةٌ
والضاحكــونَ رواسبٌ وزوائـدُ

إني أحبّـك غُصّـةً لا ترتـوي
يَفْنى الوجود وأنتَ روحٌ عاصفُ
ضَحِكــكَ جنــونٌ ودمـعٌ مُحـرِقٌ
وهـدوء قدّيسٍ وحسٌّ جـارف

إني أحبّ تعطشَ البركان فيـكَ إلى انفجـاز
وتشـوّق الليـل العميـق إلى ملاقـاة النّهـاز
وتحـرّق النبـع السخيّ إلى معانقـة الجِـراز
إني أريـدُك نهـرَ نـارٍ مـا لِلُجّتـهِ قـراز
فاغضب عـلى المـوت اللعيـنْ
إنــي مَللــت الميّتيــنْ

109

POEMS FROM
THE MOON TREE
(1968)

قصائد من
شـجرة القمـر
(١٩٦٨)

The Moon Tree

'a story I gave Maysoon when she was eleven'

I.

Atop a northern mountain clothed in pine
wrapped up in ambergris and velvet sky

where butterflies moor for the evening
and stars come down to bathe in mountain springs,

there lived a boy whose life was unlike ours.
When hungry, he ate sunset, stone and stars,

when thirsty, jasmine vines would slake his thirst,
the lively lilies were his universe.

He had strange visions, cloudy memories,
he hunted fragrant hills and melodies,

his greatest dream, though, was to catch the moon
and keep it in a cage of flowers and dew.

He spent the evenings weaving dreams and nets
head pillowed on grass cooled by rivulets,

شجرة القمر

قصة أهديت إلى ميسون يوم كانت في الحادية عشرة من عمرها

١.

على قتةٍ من جبال الشمال كَساها الصنوبر
وغلّفها أُفـقٌ مُخمـليٌ وجـوٌ مُعَنـبَر

وترسو الفراشاتُ عند ذُراها لتقضيَ المَسَاء
وعنـد ينابيعهـا تستحمُ نجـومُ السَمَاء

هنالـكَ كان يعيـشُ غـلامٌ بعيدُ الخيـال
إذا جـاعَ يأكل ضوءَ النجـومِ ولـونَ الجبـال

ويشربُ عطـرَ الصنوبرِ والياسمـين الخَضِـل
ويملأُ أفكـارَهُ مـن شَـذَى الزنبقِ المُنفعـل

وكان غلاماً غريبَ الرؤى غامض الذكريات
وكان يطـارد عطـر الـرُبَى وصَـدَى الأغنيـات

وكانت خلاصـةُ أحلامِـهِ أن يصيـدَ القَمَـر
ويودعَـهُ قصصاً مـن نـدىً وشـذىً وزَهَـر

وكان يقضّي المسـاءَ يحـوك الشبـاكَ ويَحْـلُم
يوسِّـدُهُ عُشْـبٌ بـاردٌ عند نبع مغمغِـم

113

wakeful, watching his prey's face, bright and cool
reflected in an icy, fragrant pool,

unable to sleep without moonlight's kiss
pouring the swoon of wine over his lips,

choosing to drink only from mountain streams
caressed by lace-trimmed hemlines of moonbeams.

II.

One summer, this young boy snuck out at night
barefoot, thin-blooded, and with footsteps light,

walked slowly, slowly to a towering peak
and hid his body underneath a tree,

counting the seconds with a pounding heart,
waiting for the sweet moon to rend the dark.

And all at once, the east lifted its veils,
the charming face appeared, silvery pale,

so close, and yet it did not see our hunter
as it traversed the sky in pensive wonder.

It flew right into the young lover's snare,
and once it had fallen out of the air,

ويَسْهَرُ يرمُقُ وادي المساء ووجْهَ القَمَرْ
وقـد عكستْهُ ميـاهُ غـديرٍ بَـرُودٍ عَطِـرْ

ومـا كان يغفـو إذا لم يَمُـرَّ الضيـاءُ اللذيـذْ
عـلى شَـفَتيهِ ويسقيهِ إغمـاءَ كأسٍ نبيـذْ

ومـا كان يـشربُ من منبـع المـاء إلا إذا
أراق الهلالُ عليـه غلائـلَ سكرى الشَّذَى

٢.

وفي ذات صيفٍ تسلّل هـذا الغلامُ مساءْ
خفيفَ الخُطَى ، عاريَ القدمين ، مَشُوقَ الدماءْ

وسـار وئيـداً وئيـداً إلى قمَّـةٍ شـاهقه
وخبّـأ هَيكَلَـهُ في حِـمَى دَوْحـةٍ باسقه

وراح يعُـدّ الثـوانيَ بقلـبٍ يـدُقّ يـدُقّ
وينتظـرُ القَمَـر العذْبَ والليلُ نشوانُ طَلْـقُ

وفي لحظةٍ رَفَـع الشَّرقُ أستارَهُ المُعْتمـه
ولاحَ الجبـينُ اللجينيّ والفتنـةُ المُلْهِمـه

وكان قريبـاً ولم يَـرَ صيّـادَنا البـاسِما
عـلى التـلِّ فانسابَ يذرَعُ أفْـقَ الـدُّجى حالما

the young boy marveled that the moon was his
and kissed its fragrant, butter-soft eyelids.

He took its seas of light, its tender sheen,
those lips that bring on every ancient dream,

and hid them, disbelieving, in his room.
He stared and stared – how had he caught the moon?

On splendid-scented sheets, he laid it down
and from songs, springs, and lilies wove its crown.

III.

But soon the mountain villagers caught on
and started asking where the moon had gone.

"Where are its velvet rays?" they asked, "its veils
casting their cloudy light upon our fields?"

"We want the moon!" a gang of young men cried.
"We want the moon!" the mountain peaks replied.

"Our golden night companion, our cup-bearer,
pouring the scent of flowers in our hair,

... وطوّقـهُ العاشـقُ الجبلـيَّ ومسّ جبينَـه
وقبّـلَ أهدابَـهُ الذائبـاتِ شـذىً وليونـه

وعـاد بـه: ببحـارِ الضيـاءِ، بـكأس النعومـه
بتلـك الشفـاهِ التـي شَغَلـتْ كل رؤيا قديمه

وأخفـاه في كوخـه لا يَمَـلّ إليـه النَظَـر
أذلكَ حُـلمٌ؟ وكيف وقد صاد ... صـادَ القمـز؟

وأرقَـدَه في مهـادٍ عبيريّـةِ الرّونـقِ
وكَّـلَهُ بالأغـاني، بعئينيـهِ، بالزّئبـقِ

!

٣.

وفي القريةِ الجبليّةِ، في حَلَقَـاتِ السّـمَر
وفي كّل حقـلٍ تَنَـادَى المنـادون: " أين القمر؟ "

" وأين أشـعّتُهُ المُخمليّـةُ في مَرْجِنا؟ "
" وأين غلائـلُهُ السُـحُبيّة في حقلنـا؟ "

ونادت صبـايا الجبـالِ جميعاً " نُريدُ القَمَـرْ! "
فـرّددتِ القُنَئُ السامقاتُ: " نُريـدُ القَمَـرْ "

" مُسـامِرُنا الذهـبيّ وسـاقي صدى زَهْـرِنا "
" وسـاكبُ عطرِ السـنابِل والـورد في شَعْرِنا "

watering roses, giving wounds a kiss,
caressing cold springs with butterfly lips,

lighting our reveries' way through the cold
making our braids grow long, dappled with gold.

Without the moon, how can we meet at night?
Who'll hear our songs? And who will cool our eyes?"

The lonely shepherds sang, trudging along,
arbors and valleys rustled with their songs.

But soon the villagers decided to
seek out the boy who had stolen the moon.

They pounded violently upon his door,
screaming, "We want the moon and nothing more!"

Stones, boulders, mountain paths echoed their cry,
which sprouted wings and then began to fly

to daylight's bed in carriages of rain,
filling small cups of jasmine with its flames,

gathering fortitude from nature's power,
until it had engulfed the boy's cool bower.

"مُقَبّلُ كلّ الجِراح وساقي شفاه الـوروذْ"
"وناقـلُ شـوقِ الفَـراشِ لينبـوعِ مـاءٍ بَـروذْ"

"يـضيءُ الطريـقَ إلى كلّ حُـلمٍ بعيدِ القَـرارْ"
"ويُنْـمي جدائلَنـا ويُريـقُ عليهـا النُضَـارْ"

"ومـن أينَ تـبرُدُ أهدابُنـا إن فَقَـدْنا القَمَـر؟"
"ومَنـذا يرقّقُ ألحاننـا؟ مـن يغذّي السَمَرْ؟"

ولحـنُ الرعـاةِ تـردّدَ في وحشةٍ مضنيـهْ
فضجّـتْ برجْعِ النشيـدِ العرائـشُ والأوديـه

وثـاروا وسـاروا إلى حيثُ يسكُنُ ذاكَ الغُـلامْ
ودقّوا على البـابِ في ثورةٍ ولَظًى واضطرامْ

وجُنّـوا جُنُـوناً ولم يَبْـقَ فـوق المَـراقي حجـرْ
ولا صخـرةٌ لم يُعيـدا الصُرَاخَ: "نُريـدُ القَمَـرْ"

وطـافَ الصَدَى بجناحَيْهِ حول الجبـالِ وطارْ
إلى عَـرَباتِ النجـومِ وحيثُ ينـامُ النَّهـارْ

وأشـرَبَ مـن نـارِهِ كلّ كأسٍ لزهـرةٍ فُـلّ
وأيقـظَ كلّ عبيـرٍ غريـبٍ وقطـرةِ طـلّ

وجمّعَ من سَكَراتِ الطبيعةِ صوتَ احتجاجْ
تـردّدَ عند عريـش الغُـلامِ وراء السِيـاجْ

"Why did you steal the moon?" the cry alit,
breaking the still, "Where have you hidden it?"

IV.

The boy clung to his prisoner and cried
"They'll never take you!" Tears rained from his eyes.

As shepherds' shouts cleaved through the silent still,
into a chasm of madness the boy fell

and started singing to his inspiration.
Salt tears laced hymns to beauty with emotion

until the crowd's voice, seething, wild with rage,
pierced at the boy's dream with a dagger's blade

slashed through his ears, a bullet through a bubble
reducing all his dream-castles to rubble.

Where can he run to? And where will he hide
the moon's face from the hunters' greedy eyes?

What kind of veil, oh sky, can hide its rays,
when its proud shine spoils every hiding place?

The anxious minutes passed. A knife of doubt
tore at the boy's heart, turned it inside out,

until, exasperated, wild and mad,
he took an axe into his trembling hands

وهزَّ السكونَ وصاحَ: "لماذا سَرَقْت القَمَرْ؟"
فجُرِّت المَسَاءُ ونادى: "وأينَ خَبَأَت القَمَرْ؟"

.٤

وفي الكوخِ كان الغلامُ يضُمُّ الأسيرَ الضحوك
ويُمْطِرُهُ بالدموع ويَصْرُخُ: "لن يأخذوك"

وكان هُتَافُ الرّعاةِ يشُقّ إليهِ السكونْ
فيسقُطُ من روحه في هُوَى من أسىً وجنونْ

وراح يغنّي للمِهِمِهِ في جَوىً وانْفِعَالْ
ويخلِطُ بالدّمعِ والملحِ ترنيمَهُ للجمالْ

ولكنّ صوتَ الجماهيرِ زادَ جُنوناً وثوره
وعاد يقلِّبُ حُلْمَ الغلامِ على حدِّ شفره

ويهبطُ في سَمعه كالرّصاص ثقيلَ المرورْ
ويهدمُ ما شيَّدتْهُ خيالاتُـهُ من قصورْ

وأين سيهرُبُ؟ أين يختبِّئ هـذا الجبينْ؟
ويحميهِ من سَورة الشَوقِ في أعين الصائدينْ؟

وفي أيِّ شيء يلُفّ أشعتَهُ يا سَمَاءُ؟
وأضــواؤه تتحـدّى المخابئَ في كبرياءْ؟

ومرّتْ دقائقُ منفعِلاتٌ وقلبُ الغُلامْ
تمزّقُـهُ مُدْيةُ الشكِّ في حَيْرةٍ وظلامْ

121

with all his strength, began to split the earth,
no other way – he'd bury his prisoner.

Washing the moon in tears, he said goodbye
choking, cursing his luck a thousand times.

V.

Insistent shepherds soon began to hack
at the doorjambs that fortified the shack,

until their breathless efforts finally
succeeded. They burst in – what did they see?

A shock, a disappointment – nothing there
but darkness, cold, silence filling the air,

and the young boy, immersed in dreams, asleep,
blond hair draped over hands, dream-smiling lips,

face bright with Apollonian purity,
his sleep sheer innocence, sweet reverie.

The shepherds were perplexed. Was this the thief
who'd stolen the moon and caused the world such grief?

Had they been wrong? If so, where was the moon?
The night grew dark, they left the shack confused,

وجـاء بفـأسٍ وراح يشـقّ الـثَرَى في ضَجَـرِ
ليدفِـنَ هـذا الأسـيرَ الجميلَ ، وأينَ المفرّ؟

وراحَ يودِّعُـهُ في اختنـاقٍ ويغسِـلُ لونَـهُ
بأدمعِـه ويصُبّ عـلى حظِّهِ ألفَ لعنَـهْ

٥.

وحينَ استطاعَ الرّعاةُ المُلحّـون هدْمَ الجِدازِ
وتحطيمَ بوّابةِ الكـوخ في تَعَـبٍ وانبهـازِ

تدفَّـقَ تيّـارهم في هيـاجٍ عنيفٍ ونقمـهْ
فـاذا رأوا؟ أيّ يـأسٍ عميـقٍ وأيّـة صَدْمَـهْ!

فلا شيءَ في الكوخ غيرَ السكون وغيرَ الظُلَمْ
وأمّـا الغُـلامُ فقـد نـام مستَغْرقاً في حُلُمْ

جدائلُهُ الشُـقْـرُ مُنْسدلاتٌ عـلى كَتِفيـهِ
وطيـفُ ابتسـامٍ تلـكّاً يَحلُمُ في شـفتيه

ووجهٌ كأنَّ أبولـونَ شرّبَـهُ بالوضـاءه
وإغفـاءةٌ هي سـرّ الصَفاءِ ومعنى البراءه

وحار الرّعاةُ أيسرِقُ هـذا البريءُ القَمَـرْ؟
ألم يُخطِئـوا الإتِّهـام تـرى؟ ثمّ ... أينَ القَمَـرْ؟

asking, had the moon strayed beyond the mist?
Had evil, crone-like demons hidden it

behind the clouds and smashed its countenance
into small bits for the stars' sustenance?

Had sea-waves swallowed it in salty swirls
and hidden it in palaces of pearl?

Or had the wind, her slippers worn to shreds
from wandering, gotten it in her head

to use the moon's milk-skin to make new shoes,
laced up with light? Had she stolen the moon?

VI.

Soon morning came, its footsteps damp and cold,
its dusky brow crowned with a ring of rose,

roaming the firmament with jugs of bounty,
pouring dew, cold, and light over the mountains.

It tiptoed past the boy's hut and released
a cool shower of light, dewdrops, and peace,

وعـادوا حَيـارى لأكواخهـم يسـألونَ الظـلامْ
عـن القَمَـر العبقـريّ أتاهَ وراءَ الغمـامْ؟

أم اختطفتهُ السَعالى واخفتهُ خلفَ الغيومْ
وراحـت تكسّترُهُ لتغـذّي ضيـاءَ النجـومْ؟

أمِ ابتلـعَ البحـرُ جبهتَـهُ البطّـةَ الزنبقيّـه؟
وأخفـاهُ في قلعـةٍ مـن لآلئَ بيـضٍ نقيّـه؟

أم الـريحُ لم يبـقِ طـولُ التنقّلِ مـن خُفِّها
سـوى مِـزَقٍ خَلِقـاتٍ فأخفتـهُ في كهفِها

لتصنَـعَ خُفّـينِ مـن جِلـدِهِ اللّـين اللَبَـنّيِّ
وأشرطـةً مـن سَناهُ لهيكلها الزنبـقيّ

.٦

وجـاء الصبـاحُ بليـلَ الخُطَى قـريَ البُرودْ
يتـوّجُ جَبْهَتَـهُ الغَسَــقيّةَ عِقْـدُ وُرودْ

يجـوبُ الفضـاءَ وفي كفّـه دورقٌ مـن جَمـالْ
يـرُشّ النـدى والبُرودةَ والضوءَ فوق الجبـالْ

ومـرَّ عـلى طَـرَفيْ قدَميـهِ بكـوخ الغُـلامْ
ورشَّ عليـهِ الضيـاءَ وقطّـرَ النّدى والسَّـلامْ

then moved to the foothills to do its chores,
clearing the tumult of the night before.

As if from drunken sleep, with lazy sighs,
the boy awoke – and saw, to his surprise

there in the mossy yard, where morning had
grown used to seeing dead, wind-scattered plants,

a Lote tree which had sprouted overnight,
tall tresses clothed in fertile green, so bright!

Evening had cared for it – its roots immersed
in moonlit sap drawn up from perfumed earth

grew into supple boughs scented with wine
squeezed from the moon's sweet, silver-colored light.

The boy had never seen fruits in such colors,
fit to confuse stars and make daylight jealous.

The other mountain trees were driven mad,
this new tree had borne fruits they never had.

What unreal earth, what soil, what mountain spring
had given life to such a gorgeous thing?

وراح يسـيـرُ لينجـز أعـمـالَهُ في السُـفُـوخُ
يـوزِّعُ ألوائَـهُ ويُشـيـعُ الـرِضى والوضـوخُ

وهبَّ الغـلامُ من النـوم منتعشاً في انتشـاءْ
فـاذا رأى؟ يا نَدَى ! يا شَـذَى ! يا رؤى ! يا سماءْ !

هنالكَ في الساحةِ الطُحْلُبيَّةِ ، حيثُ الصباخُ
تعـوَّدَ ألّا يَـرَى غيـرَ عُشْبٍ رَعَثـهُ الـرياخُ

هنالـكَ كانـت تقـومُ وتمتـدّ في الجـوِّ سِـدْرَه
جدائلُها كُسِيَتْ خُضْرَةً خِضْبةَ اللونِ ثَـرَّه

رعاهـا المساءُ وغذَّت شـذاها شِـفاه القَمَـرْ
وأرضَعَهـا ضوءُه المختـفي في التـرابِ العَطِـرْ

وأشـربَ أغصائَها الناعمـاتِ رحيـقَ شَـذَاهُ
وصبَّ عـلى لونِها فضَّةً عُـصِرَتْ من سَـناهُ

وأثمارهـا؟ أيِّ لـونٍ غريـبٍ وأيِّ ابتـكازْ
لقد حـار فيهـا ضيـاءُ النجـومِ وغـارَ النهـازْ

وجنَّتْ بهـا الشَـجراتُ المقلِّـدَةُ الجامِـدَه
فنـذ عصـورٍ وأثمارُهـا لم تَـزَلْ واحـده

فـمن أيِّ أرضٍ خياليَّةٍ رَضَعَـتْ ؟ أيِّ تُرْبـه
سـقتْها الجمالَ المفضَّضَ ؟ أي ينابيعَ عذْبَه؟

And then the young boy noticed with a swoon:
from every sweet, green branch, there hung a moon.

VII.

The ages passed. The village soon forgot
the wild-eyed, visionary boy and what

he'd done. Even the mountains hid his tale
forgot his songs, his footsteps, his betrayal,

and how, despite his wishes, he'd returned
the moon back to the grieving villagers.

Free in the sky, without a fixed abode,
it roams again, sprinkling dew and cold

and hints of fog in distant evenings
and echoes drawn up from cold mountain springs

whispering with the words of mossy streams
that the moon's tale was just a summer's dream.

1952

وأيــةُ معجـزةٍ لم يصِلها خَيالُ الشَـجَرْ
جميعاً؟ فمـن كلّ غُصنٍ طريّ تَـدَلَّى قَمَرْ

.٧

مـرّت عصورٌ وما عـاد أهلُ القُرى يذكرون
حياةَ الغُلام الغريبِ الرُؤى العبقريّ الجُنون

وحتى الجبـالُ طـوتْ سرّه وتناستْ خطاهُ
وأقِمـــارَهُ وأناشـــيدَهُ واندفـــاعَ مُنـــاهُ

وكيـف أعـادَ لأهلِ القُـرى الوالهِين القَمَـر
وأطلَقَـــهُ في الســَماءِ كما كانَ دونَ مقـرْ

يجـوبُ الفضـاءَ ويَنـثُرُ فيـه النَـدَى والـبُرودَه
وشِبهَ ضَبـابٍ تحـدّر مـن أمسياتٍ بعيدَه

وهَمْساً كأصداء نبـعٍ تحـدّر في عمْـقِ كثيـف
يؤكّـد أنَّ الغـــلامَ وقصّتَـهُ حُـلْمُ صيـفِ

١٩٥٢

Greetings to the Iraqi Republic

I composed this poem on the occasion of the revolution of July 14 1958.

The happiness of orphans in the arms of loving fathers
the happiness of summer when the autumn breeze
    comes back
the happiness of thirsty men who finally taste water
the happiness when rays of light illuminate the black
that is our happiness with the Republic of Iraq.

Yes, our Republic, we declare it with humility
whisper the word, caress its letters with our thirsty lips.
We have been naked, sleepless, starving, seeking
    happiness,
our dear Republic, flame of yearning and solemnity!
For years we waited, thirsty, hungry, never finding
    sleep,
feeding ourselves on dreams and never thinking we'd be
    free
now we have found you, bathed in streams of light and
    certainty.

تحية للجمهورية العراقية

نظمت هذه القصيدة تحية لثورة ١٤ تموز سنة ١٩٥٨

فَرَحُ الأيتامِ بضمةِ حبِّ أبويّه
فرحةُ عطشانٍ ذاقَ الماءُ
فرحةُ تموزَ بلَمْسِ نسائمَ ثلجيّه
فرحُ الظُلُماتِ بنبعِ ضياءُ
فرحتُنا بالجمهوريّه

جمهوريّتُنَا ، نلفظُها بهوىً وخُضُنوع
نهمسُها ، نغمُرُها قُبلاً ولهى حرّى
نلمُسُ أحرُفَها بشِفاهٍ بقيت دَهرا
تعطَشُ ، تأرقُ ، تَعرى ، وتجوعُ
جمهوريّتَنَا ، يا حُرقةَ أشواقٍ وحنينُ
نحنُ عطِشْنا لك أعواما
جُعنا وسَهِرنا ، غذَّيناها أحلاما
والآنَ ملكناها دفقةَ ضوءٍ ويقينُ

131

Our dear Republic – smiling daughter with the happy
    eyes,
we'll hold you in our arms – we have been waiting a
    long time,
watching the sleepless hills, searching on the horizon
    line –
girl with the dark hair, we will nourish you with
    lullabies.
We've harvested sharp thorns, the hatred of our
    enemies,
whose cold deceit besieged the bassinet we built for you
from nothing but our love, some shadows, a cloud of
    perfume,
we sacrificed ourselves in martyrdom to set you free.

Our dear Republic – flood of honor, brimming with
    belief
and Arab authenticity, radiant, fragrant, sweet,
honor drips from the letters of the word itself – *jumhur*
you were a dream to whose blue skies we could not find
    a door
you were burning desires veiled by clouds of fog and
    sand,
till finally we touched you with our trembling, happy
    hands.

جمهوريّتنا ، طفلتُنا الجَذلَى العينين
مولودتُنا السمراءُ الباسمةُ الشفتين
سنوسِّدُها في أذرعنا ومآقينا
سنغذِّيها بأغانينا
نحنُ ترقَّبناها زَمَناً من دون كَلالٍ
ورصَدْنا الأُفْقَ ، بَحَثنا مِلءَ روابينا
وحَصَدْنا الشوكَ ، حَصَدْنا حِقْد أعادينا
وأقَمنا مَهداً من حبٍّ وشَذَىً وظِلالٍ
كم حفَّ به كيدُ الأعداء
وسقَطْنا حولَ قوائِمِه الولى شُهداء

جمهوريتُنا دفقةُ خيرٍ مَسكوبه
تقطُرُ إيماناً وعُروبه
جمهوريتُنا ضوءٌ ، عِطرٌ ، وعذوبَه
تقطُرُ من أحرُفِها الطيبه
كانتْ حُلماً ضاعَ إلى زرقتِهِ البابُ
كانت أشواقاً مشبوبَه
يحجُبُها غيمٌ وضبَابُ
وأخيراً نحنُ لَمَسناها
بأُكُفٍ راعشةٍ فرحاً وملكناها

Our dear Republic – fragrant and intoxicating rose
kissed by the perfume of July, fulfilling all our dreams,
expectant hills and thirsty valleys dressed in festive
    clothes
to greet our new Republic, flower brushed with virtue's
    gleam.
It showers us with snow and freedom in July, brings
    back
peace, fragrance, tender visions that had come under
    attack,
Long live – we shout in song – *the new Republic of Iraq!*

Our dear Republic, spirit-rose, God keep you safe from
    harm
you were dreaming, you were a vision, but now you've
    transformed
into reality, our dearest thing in this whole world
most loved, most cherished, sweetest, softest rose,
    color of pearl.

Curl up and go to sleep, Republic-rose, behind our eyes
inside our ribs, for we have seen the many flower-
    thieves
who'll pluck and squeeze, heartlessly trading perfume –
    enemies
whose lupine longings were awakened by your fragrant
    sighs.
The market's open, rose of ours – beware its cruel jaws
stained with Zionist vengeance sought with American
    claws.

جمهوريَّتِنا وردتُنا النَشوَى العَطِره
أهداها تموزُ الطيِّبْ
أعطاها لرؤانا ، لرُبَانا المنتَظِره ،
للوادي العطشانِ المجدِبْ
وردتُنا البيضاءُ الغَضَّه
تغمرنا ثلجاً في تموزَ وحُرّيَّه
تُعطينا عطراً وسلاماً ورؤىً بَضّه
تبعثُنا أغنيةً حيّه
تحيا تحيا الجمهوريَّه

جمهوريَّتُنا وردتُنا الروحيّةُ يحُميها اللهُ
كانت حُلُماً ، كانت رؤيا
والآنَ غَدَت أغلى ما نملِكُ في الدُنيا
وأحبّ ، أعزّ ، أرقّ الوردِ وأحلاه

في أضلُعِنا يا وردتَنا الجُمْهوريَّه
في أعيُننا نامي فلُصوص الوردِ كِثَار
أعداءُ العِطرِ العابقِ ، تُجّارُ الأزهاز
أيقَظَ عِطرُكِ فيهم أشواقاً ذئبِيه
السّوقُ صَحَا يا وردُ حَذَار
من نقمتِهِ الصهيونيَّه
ومخالبِهِ الأمريكيته

Our dear Republic – rose of ours – we'll never let them
    take
the sugar we have tasted after so much deprivation.
After we bled in sacrifice to nourish liberation,
how could we now let thieves pilfer and plunder what
    we've made?
We stand ready to give you all our faith, our helping
    hands,
you've lived through tyranny and have become a
    stronger land,
we and rebirth have come with no delay – we're right
    on time.

جمهوريّتُنا ، وردتُنا ، لن نُعطيها
إنّا قد ذُقْنا سُكّرَها بعد الحرمانْ
هل نُسلِمُها لِلصِّ الآنْ ؟
جمهوريّتُنا من دمنا سنُغذّيها
نحنُ لها إيمانٌ يُعطي ويد تُنجِدْ
جمهوريتَنا عشتِ ، سَلِمْت من الطُغيانْ
إنّا والبعثَ على موعِدْ

A Song for the Arab Ruins

From Jaz', from Siqt al-Liwa,[1] and from Wadi al-Ghumar,
from Burqat Thahmad, an abode of love erased by wind
emptied of people, laid to waste, and from those ruins in
the vast Jazira, now deserted, still smelling of musk
there rose the joyous cries of ancient pasts
living eternally in watchful eyes.

These are the meadows where gazelles once grazed in bygone
   times.
The world could end, and Ya'rub's old encampments still
   would shine[2]
and smell of sweet perfume, and poetry with Arab rhymes
would still sprout fragrant buds when spring returns with
   dewy eyes.
A thousand Imru' al-Qayses mobilize
to beat back death when an abode's erased.

Sands steeped in ancient perfumes call to you, my Arab friend.
These Arab homes, in olden times, were only ever touched
by raindrop kisses, yet when you paused over them today,
you found no howdahs and no tents, no camel drivers' cries.
Their horsemen left, their melodies are gone,
cold nothingness has swallowed up their songs.

---

1   'Siqt al-Liwa' is a place-name from the opening lines of the 'hanging ode'
    (*mu'allaqah*) attributed to the ancient poet Imru' al-Qays. 'Wādī al-Ghumār'
    is a place-name from an ode by Zuhayr ibn Abī Sulmā, and 'Burqat Thahmad'
    is a place name from the *mu'allaqah* of Tarafah ibn al-'Abd.
2   Ya'rub, in addition to being the grandson of the prophet Hūd and one of the
    legendary ancient Kings of Yemen, is also 'said to have been the first person
    to speak the Arabic language.' See Stefan Sperl, *Mannerism in Arabic Poetry:
    A Structural Analysis of Selected Texts* (Cambridge, UK: Cambridge University
    Press, 1989), 209.

أغنية للأطلال العربية

ووادي الغمـار وبُرقـة ثهمَـد	مـن الجِزع من قلْب سِقط اللِوَى
وأقفَـر مـن أهـلِهِ وتَبـدّد	ومـن رَبـع نُعْمٍ عفثـهُ الـرياحُ
وما زالَ مَنبـع عطرٍ وعَسـجَد	ومـن طَلَـلٍ في الجـزيرة أقـوَى
يعيـشُ الخُلـودَ بَجفنٍ مُسَهّـد	تعالـت هُتافاتُ ماضٍ عريقٍ

سَرحَـنَ قديماً وتلـكَ الطُلـولُ	وتلـكَ المرابـعُ حيـثُ الظِباءُ
ويلبَـثُ منهـا شـذىً لا يزولُ	منـازلُ يعـرُبَ يَفْـنى الوجودُ
يَظَـلُّ يـبرعمُ مثل الفصولُ	وشِعرُ نَـدٍ عـربيَ القـوافي
ـرئ القيسِ يدفَـعُ عنها الذُبولُ	إذا دَرَسَتْ دِمنةٌ هبَّ ألفُ أمـ

مُعَطّـرةٌ بأريـجِ القِـدَم	تُنـاديـكَ يا عـربيَ رمـالٌ
قديماً سـوى قُبُـلاتِ الـدِّيَم	ديارُ العروبـة مـا لامَسَـتْها
ج؟ أين الحُـدَاءُ؟ وأين الخِيَم؟	وقفـت بهـا اليـومَ: أين المواد
أناشـيدُها وزَوَاهـا العَـدَم	تَرَحَّـلَ فرسـانُها وانطـوت

139

My Arab friend, they're foreignizing all the old abodes.
Call out to them, shed tears for them – no matter how you try,
only a frightful stillness, drowned in silence, will reply.
Foreign footsteps now desecrate the plains where oryx
    roamed
and "Tel Aviv" is written in the sands
of Bakr, Wa'il, and Nizar's old lands.[1]

A melancholy murmur rises in the quiet night
It is the barren ruins speaking, wrapped up in the pride
of old encampments and the honor of their faded stones
bearing the weight of echoed footfalls from old caravans
upon the distant, arid hills and golden, tumbling sands:
"When will you bring us back to life, o time,
when will you let our proud cortege depart?"

Listen, my Arab friend, to calls from an eternal past
and stand, bereft, beneath the stars, right where those ruins
    stand
and say, "Sand-swept Peninsula! Undying Arab ode!
tomorrow life will come to set you free
we'll bring you back with Arab unity."

1963

---

1   'Nizar' likely refers to a distant ancestor of the Prophet Muhammad; 'Bakr'
    and 'Wa'il' might refer to the Banu Bakr ibn Wa'il, an ancient Arabian tribe.

وتستعجمُ الـدارُ يا عـربي   وتُغْـرِقُ في صَمْتهـا لا تُجيبْ

فـإن تَئـكِ، تَشـتبكِ جُذرانَهـا   يردَّ عليـكَ السكونُ الرهيبْ

مَسـارحُ آرامهـا دنّسـتْها   خُطَى الوافدِ الأجنبي المُريبْ

وأرضُ نـزارٍ وبكـرٍ ووائـ   ـلَ خطّوا على رَمْلها تـلْ أبيبْ

ويَصْعَدُ في الليل همسٌ كؤيبْ   تـردّدُه الدِمَـنُ الماحله

تغلّفـهُ كـبرياءُ الطُلـولِ   وعـزّةُ أحجارها الذابله

ويُثْقِلُـه رجـعُ خطْوِ القوافـ   ـلِ في رمْلِ تلك الـرُبى القاحله

متى يا زمـانُ تعودُ الحياةُ   إلينـا وتنطلـقُ القافلَةُ؟

فيـا عـربي أُصِـخْ لنداءٍ   تَحـدّرَ مـن رَحْبَـةِ الأبديّـة

وقف حاسراً تحت ضوءِ النجوم   على رَبـعِ تلك الطلـول الأبيّـه

وقُـلْ يا رمـالَ الجـزيرةِ يا لَحـ   ـنَ ملحمـةِ العَـرَبِ الأزليّه

غداً ستعودُ إليـكِ الحيـاةُ   تعـود مـع الوَحـدةِ العربيّه

١٩٦٣

A Song for the Moon

Sumptuous glass of chilly milk or flowing stream of pearl?
White twilight painted on the cheeks of a sweet-smelling night?
A colored jar of musk dripping honey with every scoop?
Or fragrant, lily-white cheeks sleeping on cool, dewy grass?

What are you, carafe leaking light, stars melting into dark?
Lily-of-valley kisses, honey poured in pitch-black night?
Refuge of beauty, bundled blooms clutched in the sky's soft hands?
Lips made of light come down to kiss the verdant face of land?
A lake of supple jasmine poured out from the firmament?

You are the lovers' boat; you carry them on languid seas,
on feathered, wakeful wings that spread the path of love with hope.
You are a spring pouring out sleep on eyelids soft with cares,
a cupbearer for dreaming eyes, a glass of druggy sleep.
You are a finger scattering songs, a hand caressing wounds,

an island hung in darkness, its color presaging dawn,
floating above a fragrant stream with magic, starlit banks,
light frozen on its muddy edge, silk cradle, crystal trove.
You're shame's repentance and love's sail, colorful and
    soft-featured,
you're night's regret, you make amends for tornadoes and clouds.

أغنية للقمر

أم جدولٌ سائلٌ من الصَدَفِ؟	كأسُ حليبٍ مثلّجٍ تَـرِفِ
خدود ليلٍ مُعَطّرِ السُدُفِ	أم غَسَقٌ أبيضٌ يسيلُ
يقطُرُ شهداً لكلّ مُغترِفِ؟	أم حُقّ عطرٍ ملوَّنٍ خَضِلٍ
ينعَسُ فوق الأعشابِ والسَعَفِ؟	أم أنـتَ خَـدُّ مُزنبِقٌ أرِجٌ

كواكباً في الظلام مُنصَهِره؟	مـا أنتَ يا دورقَ الضياءِ ويا
شهداً مُصَفّى في ليـلةٍ عَطِرَه	يا قُبلاً سَوسنِيةً سَكبثُ
من زنبـقٍ في السماء مُنْعَصِرَه	يا مَحْبَأً للجمـالِ يا حُزَماً
تَمسَحُ وجـهَ العرائـشِ النَضِرَه	ويا شِـفاهاً مـن الضياءِ دَنَتْ
سلّة فُلٍّ في الأفُقِ منحدِره	يا بركـة العِطـرِ والنعومـة يا

عبـرَ بحارِ الأحلام والكَسَـلِ	يا زورقَ العاشـقين تحملُهُـم
يفرُشُ دربَ الغرامِ بالأمَـلِ	على جَنـاحٍ مريّـشٍ يقظٍ
ما أرّقتْـهُ الأشـواقُ مـن مُقَـلٍ	يا منبعـاً يسـكُبُ النُعاسَ على
يا كوبَ نـومٍ مخـدِّرٍ ثمِلِ	يا ساقِي الأعينِ الرقاقِ رؤىً
مُبعثَر الأغنيـاتِ والقُبَـلِ	يا أصبعـاً يلـمُسُ الجِـراحَ ويا

لَجريتـةُ اللونِ والتباشيـر	جـزيرةٌ في الدُجى معلّقـةٌ
مكوكبِ الشاطئَينِ مَسـحورِ	طافيـةٌ فـوق جـدولٍ عبِـقٍ
مهـد حريرٍ وكنّزَ بلّـور	تجمّـدَ الضـوءُ عنـد شـاطئها
مُلَـوّنٍ ناعـمِ الأساريرِ	يا توبـةَ القُبـحِ يا شِراعَ هـوىً
كَفّـارة الغيْـمِ والأعاصيـر	يا نَـدَمَ الليـلِ والظلـامِ ويا

143

Melt bits of beams and dreams in night and drown our roofs in
    silver,
shake off your wings in skies stained with color like butterflies.
Without you, shadows would not dance, the irises' tender cups
could not be chilled. You wooed our dreams and nursed us,
    beam by beam.
Small aperture of dawn inside a darkness of fatigue,

stay as you are, a secret world our souls can't comprehend,
weaver of poetry's remnants in worlds of darkened mirrors.
You make each song mellifluous by shimmering in its folds,
you give music its flavor, pulsing meter through its curves.
Stay as the fantasies sustaining life – love, poems, God.

1952

أَذِبْ شَظايا أَشِعَّةٍ ورؤُىً   في الليلِ واغمُزْ سُطوحَنا فِضَّه

وانفُضْ جناحيكَ في الفضاءِ يَسِلْ   لونُ جناحِ الفراشةِ الغَضّه

لَولاك لم تَرقُصِ الظِلالُ ولم   تبرُدْ كؤوسُ الزنابِقِ البَضّه

غزِلْتَ أحلامَنا وأرضَعَنا   ضياؤكَ العذْبُ ومضةً ومُضّه

يا كوّةَ الفَجرِ في دُجىً تَعِبٍ   يا مُطعِمَ الياسمينِ في الرَّوضه

البثُّ كما أنتَ عالمًا عجَزَتْ   أرواحُنا أن تعيَ خَفاياهُ

يا ناسِجَ الشِعرِ يا بَقيّتَهُ   في عالمٍ أظلَمَتْ مَراياهُ

أيُّ نشيدٍ لم ينبجس عَسَلاً   وأنتَ تفترّ في ثناياهُ

زنتَ منحتَ الغناءَ لذّتَهُ   يا نَبضةَ الوزنِ في حناياهُ

فأبقَ وراء الحياةِ أخيلةً   الشِعرُ فيها والحبّ واللّه

١٩٥٢

Three Communist Songs

I.

Stand up, comrade, as night falls quietly over the hills,
let's watch it closely, silently, through holes pierced in the
    dark.
Maybe the shadows are plotting secret conspiracies,
together with the starlight, scheming with the evening's still.
These hills, that road, this darkness –
they're all agents.

We'll conduct searches on sweet-smelling things, even the rain
we'll riffle through the flowers' colors and the sunlight's
    threads,
we'll expose every plot concocted by the lily-spies
and all the propaganda spread by dancing, chirping birds
We know the moon conspired with the others –
raise the scaffold!

Come, comrade, let us crush the jasmine's counter-revolution
the lily of the valley's fraud, the hateful bower's lies.
The mountain springs' cold machinations seem to know no
    end,
and this late afternoon is spreading rumors of twilight.
Beware, comrade – the rose has religion
it smells Arab.

ثلاث أغنيات شيوعية

.١

إذا نَزَل الليلُ هذي الروابي فقم يا رفيقْ
راقبُه من ثقوبِ الدُّجَى في السُّكُون العميق
لعلّ الظلامَ يُعـدّ مؤامرةً في الخفَاء
ويحبكُها مع ضوء النُّجوم وصمتِ المَسَاء
فهـذي الروابي وذاك الطريقْ
وهذا الدُّجى، كلُهُمْ عُمَلاءْ

وسـوف نفتّـشُ حـتى الأريجَ وحـتى المطـرْ
نقلِّبُ حتى خيـوطَ الضياءِ ولونَ الزَهـرْ
ونفضَـحُ مـا دبّـرتْ كلَّ جاسوسةٍ زَنْبَقـهْ
ومـا روّجَتـهُ العصافيرُ بالرَقْـصِ والزَقْزقـهْ
وإنّـا لنعـلَمُ أنَّ القَمَـرْ
تآمَـرَ فلننصبِ المِشْـنَقَهْ

رفيقي تعـالَ لنسحقَ رجعيةَ الياسمينْ
وتـزويرَ سوسنةٍ نَـذْلةٍ وعريشٍ لعـينْ
وتلـكَ الينابيـعُ إنّ دسائسَها أبديتـه
وهـذا الأصيـلُ يُذيـع أراجيفـه الغَسَقيته
حَـذَارِ رفيقي فللـوردِ دينْ
وهذا الشَـذَى روحُه عربيته

147

II.

Warm greetings, red anemones,
    greetings red sisters too,
to lips in burning colors, filled
    up to the brim with blood.

Sister, you are the noblest rose,
    symbol of blood we've shed,
your color is our hidden hate,
    you set our dreams aflame.

O banner flown over our struggle,
    noble, crimson rose,
your red is murder-colored, blood
    poured from wide open wounds.

When you thirst, we won't be stingy, sister
    with life-giving blood,
but you won't thirst, red woman,
    if there are still more to kill.

For this color, we will spill blood
    in swarming, teeming streams.
For it we would even kill spring,
    sacrifice children too.

٢.

تحيّـــــــةً شــــقائقَ النُّعمـــان
يا أختَنـا الحمـراء
يا شَــــفَةً ســـاخنة الألـــوان
مترعـــةً دمـــاءُ

أختـاهُ أنتِ أشـرفُ الـورودْ
رمزَ الدمِ المُراق
يا لـونَ مـا نُضْمِـرُ مـن حُقُـودْ
مُحرقـةِ الأشـواقْ

وردتَنــا الشريفــةَ الحمـراءْ
يا رايــةَ الكفـاحْ
يا حُمـرة القتـلِ لكِ الدمـاءْ
فارغـةَ الجِـراحْ

إن تظمـأي فبالـدمِ المُنعـشِ
أختـاهُ لا نبخـلْ
هيهـاتَ يا حمـراءُ أن تعطَشـي
وثَـمَّ مـن نَقتُـلْ

من أجل هذا اللون نُجري النجيع
جـداولاً تنثـالْ
وباسِمِـهِ نقتُـلُ حـتى الربيـعْ
ونـذبَحُ الأطفـالْ

149

Tongue licking lips now stained with blood,
    mouth burning, wanting more,
Rose of the gallows, by our hate
    we swear to keep you safe.

And here you are at the scaffold,
    so slurp from its rich hue.
Drink lots of blood and go to sleep,
    dear sister, and turn red.

يا شَـفَةً تلتظـتْ بالـدمِ
يا غـلّـةً تُحْرِقـه
بِحقـدنا نُقـسِمُ أن تَسـلي
يا وردةَ المشـنقه

والآن جئنـاكِ بـه فاحتَـسي
من لونه المُغري
دمٌ كثـيرٌ فاشْـبَعي وانْعَـسي
يا أخـتُ احمَـري

III.

Darkness, pain pricks, a scream in my ears
black winds, salty blood, salty cheeks
I buried my dagger in this boy's lungs
and clipped the rose from his face
for love of peace
but here are his remains, coming to life again,
I see him smiling, standing, dark
as thunder pounds
He is Arab ... Arab ... Arab ...

Then what? The path is laid with storms
the traitorous boy's become a swarm
boys and young men, from who knows where
brown faces watered by the sun
replacing hope with doubt and fear,
as my red dream falls to the earth in dust,
cursing their ninety million faces,
Arab, Arab, Arab faces.

1959

٣.

ظلمــةٌ، وخُــزٌّ، صُراخٌ في وجودي
الرياحُ السودُ مِلحٌ في دمي فوقَ خُدودي
خنْجري أغمدتُهُ في رئتَيِ هـذا الغُلام
وجززتُ الوردَ من خدّيْهِ حبًّا للسّلام
فإذا أشلاؤه تصحو وتحيا من جديدِ
وأراهُ بــاسماً منتصباً تحـت الظـلام
ومن الآفاق ينال دَويُ
عـربيٌّ عـربيٌّ عـربيُ

ثم ماذا؟ أصبح الدربُ أعاصيرَ وقَصْفا
الغـلامُ الأرعـنُ الغـادر قـد أصبـح ألفا
هبطــوا لم أدْرِ مــن أين: صبايا وشبابا
أوجهٌ أُسقِيتِ السُمرةَ والشمس شرابا
بَدّلــوا أمـني شُـكوكاً ومحـاذيرَ وخؤفا
وتهــاوى حُـلُي الأحمـرُ للأرض تُـرابا
لاعناً تسعين مليونَ محيًا
عربيّـاً عربيّـاً عربيّـا

١٩٥٩

POEMS FROM
FOR PRAYER AND REVOLUTION
(1978)

قصائد من
للصلاة والثورة
(١٩٧٨)

Sleeping Beauty

A word
on the page of the dictionary
is like a veiled rose
perfumes hidden, talismanic,
colors covered, like a shadow
and the word
a princess, sleeping, smiling
waiting for her lover-prince
to come from the unknown, wake summer smells
that sleepy sweet
the word
a dozing, pampered houri plucked
from heaven by the poet
shining pearl from virgin shell
in distant oceans rimmed with wandering shores
scattered like mermaids lost at sea
an unknown terrace with enchanted stones
opening a window onto spectral worlds.

What words sleep on the dictionary's sheets
their letters buds,
or wings, or suns,
or oysters hiding gems
imprisoned scents
their echoes airs from long-lost symphonies

الأميرة النائمة

يرد في قصص الأطفال أنّ أميرة مسحورة بقوة شرّيرة تنام
مائـة عـام، ويكتب لها ألّا تستفيق من نومهـا إلا إذا اقتحم
قصرها أميرٌ يحبها ويصل إليها ويقبّلها فتستيقظ.

الكلمه
في صفحة القاموس مثلُ وردةٍ ملثّمه
عطورُهَا خفيةٌ مُطَلْسمه
ألوانُها مستورةٌ، مثل الظلال المبهمه
والكلمه
أميرة نائمةٌ مبتسمه
أغفت عصوراً في انتظار العاشق الأميرْ
يأتي من المجهول، يُضْحي الصيفَ والعبيرْ
يوقظُ تلك الحُلْوَةَ المهوّمه
والكلمه
حوريةٌ، غافية، مُنعَّمه
يُخْرجها الشاعر من عُزْلتها لآلئا عُذْرية الأصدافْ
في أبحرٍ بعيدةٍ تائهة الضفافْ
ينثرها عرائساً مائية في أُفُقٍ مفقودْ
وشُرْفةً مسحورة الأستار لم يسمعْ بها الوجودْ
تفتَّحُ شباتاً على عوالم الأطيافْ

كم لفظةٍ تنامُ في القاموسْ
أحرفها براعمٌ، أجنحةٌ، شموسْ
مَحارةٌ كنوزُها مطويّه
عبيرُها محبوسْ
أصداؤها أجواءُ سمفونيته

157

one a bride
one a jinn
one an iridescent fin
one a lily
one a fruit
one an iris damp with dew
eternity, spiritual dawn
sun-kissed rebirth, unending space
lie here, forgotten on these shores.

One word a virgin, sleeping
on the banks of a canal
every letter a story
               a candle
                    a ring
one has letters made of winter
one a swoon
one brings blessings of water
one a moon
one word an ear of grain that dances barefoot through the
    grass
one echoes with the swell of desert sands
where distant windstorms hide in far-off lands.

What does the word say?
I have slept here like an orphaned girl
the dictionary page has been my bed
now who will wake me up and lift my head
tear off the veils that hide my secret world?

ولفظةٌ عروسٌ
ولفظةٌ جنّتيه
ولفظةٌ سوسنةٌ بَرّيه
ولفظةٌ شِفاهُها كؤوسٌ
ولفظةٌ تُفّاحة طريه
ولفظةٌ زنبقة مبلولة نقيّه
في شاطئيها أَبَدُ
إشراقةٌ روحيّةٌ ومَوْلدُ
ولا نهاياتٌ سَحيقات المَدَى مَنسيّه

ولفظةٌ صبيّةٌ عذراءُ
نائمةٌ على ضفاف ساقيه
فكل حرف قصّةٌ،
وشمعةٌ
وداليه
ولفظة حروفها شتاءُ
ولفظة إغماءُ
ولفظةٌ بركةُ ماءٍ صافيه
ولفظةٌ سُنْبلة ترقُصُ ما بين المروج حافيه
ولفظةٌ في رَجعها تموجُ الرمالِ في الصحراءُ
يكمُنُ فيها عَصْفُ ريحٍ نائيه

ماذا تقول الكلمه؟
في صفحة القاموس نمتُ طفلةً مشتاقةً مُتَيّمه
فمن تُرى يوقظُني لأكشف الأسرارَ؟
وأرفع الأستارَ
عن عالمٍ أبعادُهُ المُطَلْسمه
عميقةُ الأغوارُ

159

What does the word say?
I am fresh, inspired, beautiful
I'm fertile as a springtime dew
the fire's orange-red hue
sweet as prayer
murmured at the Kaaba's blessed side.
I'm perfumed like a flower bud
and give light like a burning moon,
lighting the way
for revolutionaries in the night
opening apertures of day
spicing their songs
with flowing light.

What does the word say?
I am here, in dictionary-dark
girl with a broken doll,
history hidden, orphaned ink
here I'll stay
enchanted, sleeping princess
till a poet comes
to wake me from my sleep
to bring back love and dreams
to unveil the mad histories
hidden inside my letters and my beams,
to reincarnate me in murmured song
to shower me with sprays
of fragrance and fertility
and chapters from
        an epic tale.

1973

ماذا تقول الكلمه؟
إني أنا طريةٌ ومُلهَمه
جميلةٌ وخِصبةٌ مثل نَدَى آذار
ومثل لون النار
إني أنا لذيذة مثل صلاةٍ عَذْبة مُتَمْتِمه
في الكعبة المكرّمه
إني أنا عاطرة كالبُرعُمه
إنّي أضيءُ مثلما تشتعلُ الأقمارْ
أنيرُ للثوّارْ
درب الليالي المعتمه
أفتحُ في وجوههم نافذةَ النهارْ
أرشُّ في أنغامهم طعم ضياءٍ سائلٍ
أذيب فيه نكهة البَهارْ

ماذا تقول الكلمه؟
في عَثمة القاموس أبقى طفلةً دميتُها محطّمه
تاريخها مختبئٌ، أحرُفُها مُيَتَّمه
أبقى أنا أميرةً مسحورةً منوَّمه
حتى يجيء شاعرٌ يوقظُني من غفوتي
يعيد لي حرارتي وفتنتي
يكتشف التاريخَ في حروفي الولى وفي أشعّتي
يبعثني أغنية مُغَمْغَمه
يمطرني رَشَّة خِصب وشذىً
وفِقْرةً من ملحمه

١٩٧٣

A Letter from Him

(FROM "TRILOGY AT A TIME OF PARTING WAYS," 1973)

A letter from him is rivers of green
dreams, daylight, water-wheels
I am a ship, long lost at sea
for want of a letter from him
like lips of rain
a kiss of frost on caravans
burning in desert heat
a letter comes – rose of desire, a taste of stayed-up-late
trains shelter in the stations of its words
a letter like a midnight prayer
like the Tigris glittering
in moonlit evening.

My sleepless night bites into me
as I wait for the day to bring
a letter kissed with traveling lips
and written in his hand
warm wishes for my frozen tears
its lines of text like fingers clasping mine with passion's heat
its words are lips of love, now thirsty from a night apart
its letters ears of wheat
promising soon we'll meet
the one I love and I will leave this frightening labyrinth
the shadows of this desert still.

رسالةٌ منه

من " ثلاثية في زمن الفراق "

رسالة منه نهورُ اخضرارْ
مثل الدوالي ، والرؤى ، مثل انبلاج النهارْ
رسالة أنا إليها سُفُنٌ تائهةٌ في بحارْ
تأتي إليَّ من حبيبي كشفاه المَطَر
كقبلة الثلج على قوافلٍ قد أحرَقْتها القفارُ
رسالة تأتي: ورود الشوق فيها ، ومَذَاقُ السَّهَرْ
حروفها محطة إلى مراسيها سيأوي القطارْ
رسالة مثل صلاة الوَتَرْ
مثل انهار دجلةٍ في أمسيات القَمَرْ

تمضَغُني ليلتي الساهده
أنتظر الصباح يأتيني بها ، بالشّفة الوافده
رسالةٌ من يده ، دفءُ مُنئ لأدمعي البارده
سطورها أصابعٌ تحوي يدي في وَلَهٍ واحتراقْ
ألفاظُها شفاهُ حبٍّ عطشت وراء ليل الفراقْ
حروفها سنابلي الواعده
بأننا سنلتقي عن قريبْ
أنا ومن أحبّهُ ، نخرجُ من هذا المتاه الرهيبْ
من ظُلُمات هذه المفازة الراكده

163

After a long, perplexing trip
through barren dark
mountains of thirst
summits erased, hills of anticipation
my dreamed-of train approaches terraced homes
takes shelter in a station made of stars and storming rain
of silver, electricity, and spice
of warm perfume.

بعد رحيلٍ شاسع ذاهلِ
بعد دُجئ ماحلِ
بعد روابي الظمأ القاتلِ
بعد ذرئ ممحوةٍ ، بعد تلال انتظارْ
قطار أحلامي يُداني شُرُفاتِ الديارْ
يأوي إلى محطّةٍ من أنجم ، من مطرٍ هاطلِ
من فضّة ، من كهربٍ ، من بَهَارْ
ومن عبير دافئ سائلِ

A Letter to Him

(FROM "TRILOGY AT A TIME OF PARTING WAYS," 1973)

With longing washing over me
I water it
I water it
in dreams, in my expansive wakefulness
I water it
I feed it tears like grapes,
give it the rhythm of escape
and homes in all the cities of my heart,
so that my lips, my poems, boats and roads
no longer gnaw at it.

I'll plunge its lines into an inkwell filled with tears and blood
I'll punctuate it with a pen I fashioned from my ribs
I'll lose myself in spaces till I can't tell east from west
I'll break my oar and put to sea
without a sail
my ropes plucked eyelashes
my mast a flag of love
plunged into clouds of woe.
Part, part, you waves
show me a witch, a mermaid's flashing scales
to soothe these wounds and tears
and let me fly like lightning to the shore,
to harvest plants and stars.

To my lover I write
under cover of night
when darkness is a wild dog crouched beside me, and wind blows

رسالة إليه

من "ثلاثية في زمن الفراق"

أسقيها من موجة شوقي
أبقَى أسقي
في حُلمي ، ومسافة صحوي
أسقي أسقي
أطعِمها أعنابَ دموعي
أمنَحُها إيقاعَ خُشوعي
أسكنها كلَّ مدائن قلبي ، لا أُبقي
أُمضغها شفتي ، أشعاري ، سُفُني ، طُرُقي

سأغتس أسطُرَها بدواةٍ من عَبَراتي ونجيعي
وفواصلُها سوف تضيِّعُني لا أعرف غربي من شرقي
ينكسرُ المجدافُ وأُبحر دون قلوعِ
حَبلي من هُدُبي المنزوعِ
صاريتي غيمة أحزان ، بيرقُ شوقِ
يا أمواجُ انشقِّي ، انشقِّي
عن ساحرةٍ وعروس بحورٍ
تمسَحُ جُرحي ودموعي
تضمنُ أن أعبر كالبَرْق
للشاطئ ، حيث حَصَادُ نجومي وزروعي

لحبيبي أكتب تحت الليل رسالة حُبْ
والظلمةُ كلبٌ وحشيٌ يجثم قربي ، والريح تَهُبْ

Should I write with my mouth? This mouth?
Pour out my flames
    my pains
        the screaming sound inside my blood
    onto its page?
Should I depict my love? my sleeplessness?
the evening's ash?
or water it with ink-tears as they
plop out from my pen?
should I strew my soul's ruins, scatter my body's remains
over the valleys of the page?

No, no, it's not enough
none of this is enough
I'll be the words, I'll hide inside their ink
I'll be the mailman too
my eyelash or my arm will be the stamp
I'll write the address: Lovers' Building, Street of Beating
    Hearts
Return address? Madwoman Trapped Inside a Labyrinth
across a rainless, lightless, empty waste
I'll send my mail by air, so let the cold wind claw at me
let my ten fingers freeze
I will defy my veins and kill my fear,
I will battle my weakness – let the dark envelop me
love is my lantern and my stars
and when the winter blankets me
your face bidding farewell
is summer heat.
Let all my limbs turn into clay – love is my animating breath.
Give my skies cloudy faces
which your love clears as it pours
an open door

هل أكتبها بفمي؟ بفمي؟
أأريقُ على الصفحاتِ حُرُوقي؟
إعصاري؟
وَصُراخَ دمي؟

أأصوّر شوقي أم أَرَقي؟
ورمادَ مسائي المحترق؟
أم أسقيها عبراتٍ تنزفُ من قَلَبي؟
تذرو أنقاضي وخرائبَ، روحي في أودية الوَرَق؟

كلا، لا يكفي، لا يكفي
سأكونُ أنا الكلماتِ، سأكمُنُ في الحَرُفِ
سأكون إليه أنا (الساعي)
و(الطابع) هُدُبي وذراعي
و(العنوان): عمارة حبّي
شارع قلبي
و(المرسلة) الولهى المسجونةُ خلف متاهات الأبعادْ
عبر الصحراء بلا مطرٍ يشدو، وبلا ضوءٍ لا زادْ
وبريدي جَوِّيٌّ فلتخدشْني الريحُ
ولتجمُدْ من بردِ كفي
إني أتحدّى أوردتي، أقتُلُ خوفي
أصرع ضعفي
ولتحلُكْ ظُلُماتي فالشوقُ مصابيحُ
ونجومٌ، وهواي فسيحُ
وشتاءٌ حولي ووداعةُ وجهكَ صيفي
ولَيكُ أجوائي غامضةُ الجبهه
إنَّ هواكَ وضوحُ
والظلمة بابٌ مفتوح

I'll go down to the street of beating hearts
I'll humbly circumambulate the building of my love
the stairs are my night-journey, the apartment my mihrab
I'll knock and knock and knock upon the door –
"Open, my love
dearer than all –
a letter of desire and flesh
of nerves, a dancing heart, and bone
has come to you across the sky
it has a mouth that trembles with your name
your name, your name, your name, your name
from balconies of air
    the clouds' hair
come get your mail
my light!
    my pride!
        my shining star!"

October 4 1973

وسأهبط في شارع قلبي
وأطوّفُ خاشعةً حول عمارة حبّي
السُّلَّم مِعُراجي ، والشقّة لي محرابُ
وأدقُّ ، أدقُّ ، أدقُّ البابُ
افتح يا من هو أغلى من كل الأحباب
لكَ عبر الجوّ رسالةُ شوقٍ من لحمٍ
من أعصابٍ ، من قلبٍ يرقُصُ ، من عظمٍ
ولما شَفَةٌ تنبِضُ باسمكَ
باسمكَ ، باسمكَ ، باسمكَ ، باسمكَ
فتلقَّ بريدك من شرفاتِ الليلِ ،

ومن شَعُر الغيمِ

يا ضنوئي!

يا عطري!

يا مجدي!

يا نجمي!

٨ رمضان ١٣٧٣ هـ ــ ١٩٧٣/١٠/٤م

Headlines and Advertisements in an Arab Newspaper

Sidon passes a terrifying night.
A new, expanded map
of enemy lands. Golda declares that Israel will never bend
she'll track the Fedayeen.
Lebanon crumbles from the south. Impending
siege on the canal.
Ladies! What will you wear
to the evening's soirée? In what sash will you make your first
    appearance?
Ladies! Be young, stormy, and hot,
use these perfumes from Paris, sip our wine
it's sprinkled with the scents and tears of spring.
Enjoy yourself! Your life is passing fast,
you're wrinkling up and growing old,
and wine, dear Madam, is lilies and figs.

Brezhnev smiling at Nixon with
good tidings of a new world order.
New settlements along the Jordanian border.
Ladies! Paint your long nails in crimson hues
so sleek and smooth
like the drowned echo of an organ's murmur.
Jews come from Moscow to Jerusalem
tax-free.

عناوين وإعلانات في جريدة عربية

صيدا تقضّي ليلةً مروّعه
خريطةٌ جديدة موسَّعه
لدولة العدوِّ. غولدا صرَّحت بأن إسرائيل لن تلين
بأنها ستقتفي خُطَى الفدائيين
تسقيهمو من كأسِ موتٍ مُترَعه
لبنانُ ينهارُ جنوناً. غارةٌ
فوق القِنال مُزْمَعَه
سيّدتي ماذا ستلبسين؟
في سهرة الليلة في أيِّ وشاح سوف تظهرين؟
سيّدتي كوني شباباً ساخناً وزوبعه
استعملي عطور باريسَ اكري من خمرِنا المشعشعه
فخمرُنَا قد قطَّر الربيعُ فيها عطرَهُ وأدْمُعَه
تمتَّعي فالعمر يمضي راكضاً، والسَنَواتُ مُشرَعه
وأنتِ تهرمين
والخمر يا سيّدتي زنابقٌ وتين

بريجنيف باسمِ لنكسِنِ
بُشرى غدٍ للعالمينَ عاطرٍ ملوّنِ
مستعمراتٌ جُدُدٌ سُتُبْتَنَى على حدود الأردنِ
أظفارك الطوال يا سيّدتي اطليها
بصبغ قرمزيٍّ ليّنِ
كأنه رجعٌ غريقٌ ذاهلٌ من تمتمات أرغنِ
يهاجر اليهودُ من موسكو—ويُعْفَوْن من الضريبه—
لأورشليمَ الحلوةِ الحبيبه

173

A dancer at the Pelican was like a mellifluous song,
Small towns in Southern Lebanon are terrified
their roads cut off
corpses flung into graves
houses in ruin, laid to waste.
A dancer at the Pelican
was lithe like grapes on ripened vines
her cheeks stained blush
how young and fresh!
how small her waist!

A new song by Najat
tonight, a magical soiree with ten professional dancers
naked and drunk
those who can't come
are missing out, glass after glass until we reel
until the music swells
until we've freed ourselves from Israel.
We've paved the way to freedom with these songs
tomorrow we'll return
to Palestine. With wine we'll free the land we lost.
Tonight, the enemies' elites, together with armed guards
will animate a million sweet soirées
while Phantom fighter jets break barriers of sound
     scarring our skies, happily rushing home.

راقصةٌ في مسرح البَجْعة كالأغنية المسكوبه
جَنُوبُ لبنانَ قُرًى مُرَوَّعه
أوصالُها مُقَطَّعه
سُكَّانُها إلى القبور جُثَثٌ مشيَّعه
بيوتُهم خرائبُ منثورةٌ، أعمدةٌ مُخَلَّعه
حرائقُ مُنْدلعه
راقصةُ البجعة مَيْساءُ كأغصان الكروم الممرعه
خدودها من خمرةٍ مبقّعة
شبابُها ما أروعَهُ!
وخصرُها ما أبدَعَهُ!

أغنيةٌ جديدةٌ تُنْشدها نجاةُ
هذا المساءَ، حفلةٌ ساهرةٌ وعَشْرُ راقصاتْ
عُزِيٌّ وخمرٌ، خاسرٌ مَنْ لم يَذُقْ
الكأس تلو الكأس حتى يترنَّح الأُفُقْ
حتى نكونَ قد تخلَّصنا من اليهودْ
وبالأغاني قد رصفنا دربنا الحرَّ، غداً نعودْ
إلى فلسطينَ فبالكؤوس حرَّرنا ترابَ الوطن المفقودْ
في هذه الليلة، تُحْيَى سَهَراتٌ ممتعه
نهب العدوَّ نخب آليَّاتِهِ المدرَّعه
وطائراتُ فانتومٍ تخرق بُجُبَ الصوت في سمائنا
ثم تعودُ فرحةً مندفعه

175

America feeds Tel Aviv
stockpiles of Arab Unity
and Lebanon's a lost child with pale cheeks
its words tremble and burn, it seeks
food aid from the U.N., it cries
sheds everything it has in tears
broadcasts the enemy's attacks
and begs the stoic U.N. to act
but America is Mistress of the Veto
and as for us
their threats still rend our tents.
Our only weapons are our ranting, braying, useless words
our shame cries meekly from its cage inside enemy hands
    it surges in our veins
our necks are still exposed, laid out under Israeli knives
Al-Wadi restaurant is offering new alcohols
and Men! As you hunt down the one you love, woman or girl
the strongest governments protect us, whatever we do
they're vigilant
they're working to restore
the lands we lost.

The Arab man still summers for four months out of the year
his plan this morning is a sailing trip
and then an evening at the old Auberge
with song and dance
glasses of wine
the tender, warm, flabby embrace
of a feminine face
whose eyes make disobeying sweet.

أمريكةٌ تدعم تل أبيبَ من أرصدة العروبة المجمَّعه
لبنانُ طفل ضائع ، خدودُهُ ممتقعه
ألفاظُهُ راعشةٌ متّقده
ويستجيرُ كلَّ يوم صارخاً بالأم المتحده
يصبُّ ما بين يَدَيْها أدمعَهْ
يشكو لها ما يصنَعُ العدوّ يرجوها سدىً أن تمنعه
يسألُها أن تَصفَعَهُ
أمريكة سيّدة الفيتو ونحنُ لم تزل خيامنا مهدّده
سلاحنا ألفاظنا الهادرة المعربده
ذلّتنا بين يَدَيْ عدوّنا تصيح في عيوننا
تضجُّ ملء الأورده
ولم تزل أعناقُنا تحت سكاكين اليهود
لم تزل ممدّده
في مطعم الوادي خمورٌ جيّده
يا سيّدي وتنتقي من تشتي : آنسةً أو سيّده
ونحن تحمينا حكوماتٌ شِدادٌ وَرِعه
تسهَرُ طولَ ليلها ،
تعمل لاسترجاع كلِّ قريةٍ مُضَيَّعه

والعربيُّ لم يزل يصطافُ في العام شُهوراً أربعه
منهجُهُ هذا الصباحَ رحلةٌ نهريّة وأشرعه
والأمسيه
في مسرح الأوبيرج بين رقصة وأغنيه
حول الكؤوس المُنسِيَه
بين ذراعَيْ بضّةٍ مُسترخيه
دافئةٍ من أجل عينيها تطيبُ المعصيه

Old newspapers of every kind
opportunists toeing the line
between what's true and false
the headlines echo with a rumbling sound
and then dissolve
in seconds as the storm subsides.

Cairo, 19 Rajab 1393 / August 17 1973

جرائدٌ منوّعه
ما بين حدّ الحقّ والباطل تبقى إتمعه
وللعناوين صَدَىً وقرقعه
ثم تذوبُ في ثوانٍ ، تتلاشى الزوبعه

القاهرة في ١٩ رجب ١٣٩٣ هـ   ١٩٧٣/٨/١٧ م

POEM FROM
THE SEA CHANGES ITS COLORS
(1977)

قصيدة من
يُغير ألوانه البحر
(۱۹۷۷)

And We Still Have the Sea

we stood by the sea in the midday heat, two excited kids
my spirit swimming through your fields
    flooded rivers of your eyes
my heart chasing the question
whose buds perfume your lips

your question is sweet as a cold north wind
as splendid as songs from lovesick violins
hidden inside your hands
your question shines sky-colored onto trellises and ponds
you asked about the sea,
do its colors change?
are its waves different shades?
do its shorelines shift?

you asked, your eyes as wide as dreams
your face a distant star
lost ship without a port
you asked, your lashes ears of wheat
a field that swells in waves,
the wonder of a child
your hands the flowing sails
on two boats
sent out beyond the distance,
past what we can see
and I said, yes,
my love
the sea changes its colors
green ships surge across it
pale cities rise from it

ويبقى لنا البحر

وقفنا على البحر تحت الظهيرة طفلين منفعليْن
وروحي يسبح ، عبر مروجكَ ،
في نهر عينين مغدقتين
وقلبي يركض خلف سؤالٍ
حملت براعمه عطر مرعئ ، على شفتيك

سؤالُكَ فيه عذوبةُ ريح الشمالِ
وروعة أغنية سكبتها كنجات شوق مخبأة في يديك
سؤالُكَ لونُ سماء على برِك ودوالي
سألت عن البحر هل تتغيّر ألوانُهُ؟
وهل تتلون أمواجُهُ؟ هل ترى تتبدلُ شطآنه؟

سألتْ وعيناك واسعتان اتّساع الرؤى
ووجهك نجمٌ نأى
وسُفْنُ مضيّعة لم تجد مرفأ
سألت وهدبُكَ دهشةُ طفلٍ
ورعشةُ سنبلة ، وتموّج حقلٍ
وكانت يداكَ شراعين منهمريْن
على زورقيْن
وراء المدى والرؤى شارديْن
وقلتُ ، نعم ، يا حبيبي
يغيّر ألوانه البحرُ ،
تعبر فيه سفائنُ خُضْرُ
وتطلق منه مدائنُ شُقْرُ

and sometimes it drinks the sunset's blood
and sometimes it turns the color of sky
and gathers its blue, my love, and dreams,
gazing with sprayed,
celestial eyes
into the void, turning the shade
of morning light
and dims its chandelier at night

you asked about the sea, do its colors change?
are its waves different shades? do its shorelines shift?
yes, my love,
a sea laps at the edges of my soul's ravine
travels lonely through deserted fields
and colored harbors with their sunny sheen
a moonlit twilight bathes in its waves
wetting its hair
and tosses down a portion of its dreamy, twinkling sky
yes, my love, yes, the sea colors its gulfs
yes, the sea changes colors,
it drinks the yellow of my uncertainty
it takes on the blue tone of my melody
as my songs and ships set sail on its scattered waves
it turns white, seafloor bright
as a new jasmine bloom
it turns green, with the green
of the saddest of eyes
like the peridot waters of old Nahavand
in the depths of my grief.

do you ask of the sea, and if its colors change
when your eyes are a sea, stretching out
    till its edges are lost

ويشربُ حيناً دماءَ الغروبِ
ويصبح حيناً بلونِ الفضاءْ
يلملم زرقتَهُ يا حبيبي
ويحلم ، يرنو بعينينِ شذريتينِ
سماويتينِ
إلى اللانهاية ، يأخذُ لونَ الضياءْ
صباحاً ويُطفئ كلَّ ثرياتِه في المساءْ

سألتَ عن البحرِ ، هل تتغير ألوانُهُ؟
وهل تتلونُ أمواجُهُ؟ هل ترى تتبدل شطآنُهُ؟
نعم يا حبيبي ،
وبحرُ يلاطم وديانَ نفسي
ويرحَلُ عبر موانئ لونٍ وشمسٍ
وعبر حقول مغيبٍ
ويغتَسل الغسق القمريُّ بأمواجه ويبلّل شعرَه
ويُلقي إليه سماءً وفكره
نعم يا حبيبي ، نعم ، ويلوّن خلجانَهُ
نعم ويغيّر ألوانَهُ
فيشربُ صُفرة شكّي وظنّي
ويصبح أزرق في لون لحني
وتُبحِر في شذر أمواجه أغنياتي وسُفني
ويصبح أبيَض ، تصبح لجّتُهُ ياسمينه
ويصبح أخضَر ، مثل اخضرار العيون الحزينه
ومثل زبرجد نهر النهاوند في قعر حزني

سألتَ عن البحرِ ! هل تتغير ألوانُهُ؟
وعيناكَ بحر ترامى وضاعتْ
حدود مداهُ وشطآنُهُ

185

yes, my love, the sea changes its colors and turns ashy-gray
and tastes just like a night when sleep stayed far away
all its fish made of ash,
                              pearls
                                    sponge
                                           octopus
                                                  ash
and its sunken metropolises with drowned domes
are ash too, as the ashen color on the face
of a drowned man who floats,
pillowed on salty waves,
unconscious, drinking water
whose salt is cruel nightshade and ash on his lips
my ocean, your ocean, this ocean of ash
has a heart
and a harshness that slaps at the corpse,
spreading out, pillow-soft
as my sea and your sea picks a fight with the body
gray-colored and drowned
    sends a cruel wave to strike him
and mermaids to bear him
    to sands of forgetting, like wine
he lies on the shore, senseless and inert
    and the sea made of ash
sprays his motionless form, and a wave full of love
sweetly plays on his cheeks, washing them, till his face
glistens, sparkling with love and sea salt and white foam
        now it covers the corpse
now returns, now retreats, now it leaves the body
to numb eternity

نعم يا حبيبي ، يغيّر ألوانَهُ ويصير بلون الرماذْ
له كل طعم ليالي السهاذْ
وماديةٌ كل أسماكه ، ورَمَاذْ
لآليه
اسفنجُهُ
اخطبوطاتُهُ ، ورماذ
مدائنه الغارقات القباب ، ولونُ الرماذ
جبين غريق طفا وتوسّدَ أمواجَهُ الملح ، مغمئ عليهْ
ويبتلع الماء ، والملح عوسجةٌ ورماد على شفتيهْ
وبحري وبحرك ، بحرُ الرماذْ
حنونُ الفؤاد
له قسوةٌ تلثُمُ الجرحَ ، تفرش لينْ وساذْ
وبحري وبحرك شاكس جسم الغريق الرماديّ
ارسل موجتَهُ القاسيه
لتلطمه ، وعروس بحور لتحملَهُ
للرمال النبيذية الناسيه
ويرقد من دون وعي على الجرف ، مغمئ عليه ،
وبحر الرماذ
يرشرش اغماءَهُ ، والشبابُ الغريقْ
تغازل خدّيه ، موجة حبّ ، وتغسل جبهتَهُ وتريقْ
عليه المحبّة والملح والرغو ...
حيناً يغطّي الجَسَدْ
وحيناً يعود ويرتدُّ عنه ، ويتركُهُ لذهول الأبد

you who ask me:
    does my sea and your sea change its colors?
does it paint its shores in oils and coal
like the clouds?
my love,
in my youth my grandfather
was tall, long, and strong, like hair braided in spring
he had depth
              shadow
                     breadth
and the strength of a storm
he was wise as an edgeless and enchanted sea
and as strong as a wave

when one day tongues of flame
crept their way to our house, gnawed at walls
and set curtains alight
as the flames turned in circles on dream-balconies,
and made light of our terror
and threatened to spread
through the whole neighborhood
vowed to eat cheeks
                lips
                   doors
and even the straw on the threshing-floors

my grandfather rushed at it, rash as a wave
cried out loudly in fright
with a tornado's rage
and charged at the fire with curses and swears
insults, rain, and compassion
ferocity singing like a line of verse,

ويا من تسائلني :

هل يغيّر بحري وبحرُكَ ألوانَهُ ؟

ومثل الغيوم يلوّنُ ، يرسمُ ، بالزيت والفحم شطآنَه ؟

حبيبي لقد كان لي في الطفولة جَدُّ

طويل كمثل جدائل شعرٍ ربيعٍ وريفْ

وكان لجدّي عمق ،

وظلّ

وبُعْدُ

له عنفُ عاصفة في خريفْ

وكان مدىً في بحار مطلسمةٍ لا تُحَدُّ

وجدّيَ كان قوياً كموجة بحر مخيف

وفي ذات يوم سَرَتْ ألسن النار في بيتنا

مضت تمضغ الباب ، تُشعل لين الستائرْ

يدور اللهيبُ دوائرْ

يزمجر في شُرَفات مُنانا ، ويضحك من رعبنا

يهدّد أن يتوسّع ، يركض في حيّنا

وينذر أن يتغدّى خدوداً ،

شفاهاً ،

ظفائر

ويغتال حتى شباب البيادرْ

وأقبل جدّي مندفعاً مثل موجة بحرٍ

وأرسل صيحة هولٍ وذُعْرٍ

تحدّر في عنف إعصار نوءٍ ، يسبُّ ويلعنُ

شتائمه مطر وحنانٌ ، شراستُهُ بيت شعر مُلَحَّنْ

189

morning star, praying lips
perfume skiff
the abuse on his tongue like a colorful stream
and my grandfather put out the fire
saved my lashes and hair from the flames

my love—my grandfather was also a sea
changing colors, stone quarries for eyes, black and green
changing waves, reaching past the horizon, and fashioning
    pearls
making springs flow, and mooring on shores
creating new distances, scattering isles
spraying golden sand islands across the gulf's blue
and his buckets of curses were vials of cool balm
breaking bracelets of fire from wrists and forearms

the strength of the waves in my sea and your sea
has transformed into hands and a chest
to carry the gray body of the drowned man
to rain down on it kisses and love
lay it gently on safety's shores
with the fluttering wings of a dove

and give him new life
    sow his death with dreams sweet
        and with memory's wheat
and the cold of a cloud

وهمسُ صلاةٍ ، ونجمة فجرٍ
وزورق عطرٍ
ومدُّ السباب على شفتيه غديرٌ ملوّنُ
وأطفأ جدّي الحريق ، وانقذ هدبي وشعري

حبيبي ، وجدّي قد كان بحرا
يغيّر ألوانَهُ وتصير محاجر عينيه سوداً وخُضْرا
يبدّل أمواجه ، يترامى ، يصوغ لآلئ
يُسيل ينابيعَ ، يرسي شواطئ
ويبدع مدّاً ، ويصنع جَزْرا
يبعثر عبر ازرقاق الخليج جزائر شُقْرا
وكانت جرادله وهي تلعن ، كانت قمامٌ بلُسَمٍ
تكتّر أسورة النار ، عن ساعدٍ ليّنٍ وذراع ومعصمٍ

وقسوة أمواج بحري وبحرك صارت اكفّاً وصدرا
لتحمل جسم الغريق الرماديّ تمطره قُبَلاتٍ وزهرا
وترميه فوق ضفاف السلامه
رفيف جناح حمامه

وتعطيه عمراً جديداً
وتزرع إغماءَهُ حُلُماً
وسنابل ذكرى
وبردَ غمامَه

191

how can you ask me
of color and the sea, my love,
   when you are my sail
   and the hues of my sea
      and the dream-filled stupor in my eyes
when you are the mist on my paths
my sails
   when you are the peaks of my waves
sad rose sprung from my grief
sweet scent of my pale skin?

you ask me of color and the sea, my love
but you are my seas
my pearl and my shell
and your face is my home
so carry my boat
on a wave of desire, hidden and enclosed
to a dark and impossible shore
   with no flatlands, no hills
to a twilight with moonlit expanses
so deep
colorless in the day
branchless in forests thick
free of terror and hope

we will lose ourselves there
eating warmth in the winter, plucking snow in spring
praising frost for its wool
where shadows have no shape

عن اللونِ والبحر تسألني يا حبيبي؟
وانت شراعي،
وألوان بحري
وغيبوبة الحُلم في مقلتي
وأنت ضباب دروبي
وأنت قلوعي
وأنتَ ذُرَى موجتي
ووردة حزني، وعطر شحوبي

عن اللونِ والبحر تسألني يا حبيبي
وأنت بحاري
ومرجانتي ومحاري
ووجهك داري
فخذ زورقي فوق موجة شوقٍ مغلّفةٍ، خافيه
إلى شاطئ مبهم مستحيلٍ،
فلا فيه سهلٌ ولا رابيه
إلى غَسَق قمريّ المدارِ
عميق القرارِ
وليس له في الظهيرة لونُ
وليس له في الكثافة غُصنُ
ولا فيه هولٌ، ولا فيه أمنُ

هنالك سوف نضيعْ
ونأكل دفء الشتاءِ، ونقطف ثلج الربيعْ
ونغزل صوف الصقيع
هناك لا طول للظل في حُلمنا لاقِصَر

193

where fate has no ledger
and glances raise nothing
but songwaves descending
from mountains of moon

we laugh we cry your eyes
reflect the color of the sea
we still have color
             sea
                eternity.

15 Jumada al-Akhira 1394 / July 5 1974

ولا دفتر للقدر
ولا شيء يمكن أن يرتقيه النَظَر
سوى موج أغنية تتحدر عبر جبال القَمَر

ونضحكُ نبكي وعيناك تعكس لون البحر
ويبقى لنا اللونُ ،
والبحرُ ،
والأبد المنتظَر

١٥ جمادى الآخر ١٣٩٤ / ٥ – ٧ – ١٩٧٤

195

ACKNOWLEDGMENTS

This book would not have been possible without the generous support of a PEN/Heim Translation Fund Grant. I would like to express my sincerest appreciation to PEN (and to the endowment given by Michael Henry Heim and Priscilla Heim), and I encourage other emerging translators to apply for this unique opportunity.

Thank you also to Professor Ferial Ghazoul, who not only clarified the copyright status of Malā'ikah's work, but also moved heaven and earth to put me in touch with the Malā'ikah family and ensure their support of this project.

My thanks also Barrāq Maḥbūbah, the son of Nāzik al-Malā'ikah and her husband 'Abd al-Hādī Maḥbūbah, for generously granting me the permission to publish this work. Thanks also to others in the extended family, particularly Maysoon Malak and Nesreen Melek.

I am also grateful to Professor Abdulwahid Lu'lu'a and Professor Salih J. Altoma, who generously shared their decades of scholarship on Iraqi poetry. A thousand thanks also to Qussay al-Attabi and Sinan Antoon, who patiently answered my questions, read the poems with extreme care, and offered invaluable suggestions.

I'd also like to sincerely thank Lynn Gaspard at Saqi Books for her incomparable patience as an editor, and for taking an interest in *Revolt* when it was only a glimmer in my eye. Alexander Key also supported this work from its earliest stages, and the seminar he organized at the 2018 American Comparative Literature Association Annual Meeting helped me think about poetic translation from Arabic (and Persian) in new ways. Thanks also to the other participants in that seminar: Michael Cooperson, Terri de Young, Aria Fani, Maziyar Faridi,

Domenico Ingenito, Alexander Jabbari, David Larsen, Paul Losensky, Rawad Wehbe, and Alan Williams; I learned a great deal from our conversations. I also presented translations-in-progress at an earlier ACLA seminar organized by Hager Ben Driss, Mona Kareem, Nancy Linthicum, Imed Nsiri, and Rania Said, whom I thank for their thoughts and reflections.

To friends, colleagues, and supporters both near and far who listened and advised – Shahzad Bashir, Elliott Colla, Robyn Creswell, Harris Feinsod, Forrest Gander, Kenneth Haynes, Elias Muhanna, Sawako Nakayasu, Holly Shaffer – the words 'thank you' are never enough.

And to Levi Thompson, the first and last reader, endless thanks. I dedicate this book, and anything good that might be in it, to him.